THE WIZARD'S
GIFT

First published by O Books, 2008
O Books is an imprint of John Hunt Publishing
Ltd., The Bothy, Deershot Lodge, Park Lane,
Ropley, Hants, SO24 0BE, UK
office1@o-books.net
www.o-books.net

Distribution in:

UK and Europe
Orca Book Services
orders@orcabookservices.co.uk
Tel: 01202 665432 Fax: 01202 666219 Int. code
(44)

USA and Canada
NBN
custserv@nbnbooks.com
Tel: 1 800 462 6420 Fax: 1 800 338 4550

Australia and New Zealand
Brumby Books
sales@brumbybooks.com.au
Tel: 61 3 9761 5535 Fax: 61 3 9761 7095

Far East (offices in Singapore, Thailand, Hong
Kong, Taiwan)
Pansing Distribution Pte Ltd
kemal@pansing.com
Tel: 65 6319 9939 Fax: 65 6462 5761

South Africa
Alternative Books
altbook@peterhyde.co.za
Tel: 021 447 5300 Fax: 021 447 1430

Text copyright Mark Townsend 2008

Design: Stuart Davies

ISBN: 978 1 84694 039 2

A CIP catalogue record for this book is available
from the British Library.

Printed in the US by Maple Vail

THE WIZARD'S GIFT

By Mark Townsend

BOOKS

Winchester, UK
Washington, USA

CONTENTS

To all my parents, blood, step and in-law:
Pennie and Mike, Tim and Cheryl, Paul and Chris.

'You are unique, you are beautiful, you were made in Heaven,
there is no-one like you, you are special, you are once only,
you are never to be repeated, you are incredible,
you are a Wizard!'

PREFACE

The author lives within two worlds – the world of religion and the world of magic. The further his journey takes him the more he realizes that they are not two worlds... but one.

Note: No character is based on any real person, neither is the church fellowship that is mentioned throughout. Any possible correlations are therefore totally accidental!

ACKNOWLEDGMENTS

Jodie, who had to listen to my story unfold (literally), Aisha and Jamie who had to suffer their dad living in a cloud during its writing. Kenton Knepper, Enrique Enriquez and all other members of the S.E.C.R.E.T SCHOOL. Romany Diva of Magic, Eugene Burger, Jeff McBride, Robert E Neale, Richard Taylor, Carver and Coppersmith, for allowing me to photograph his wonderful Reading Chair and Green Man. And my brother James Townsend, for taking the excellent photograph!

FOREWORD

'A WIZARD COMMENTS'

I am honoured to say a few words about Mark Townsend's book The Wizard's Gift. I was asked to do so as I am a real life Wizard of a certain breed, and Mark a student of mine. We are magical performers, magician and mentalist, as well as having a more esoteric lineage. Perhaps that gives you fair warning that what follows is not the common fare.

Wizards are very much into the proper blending of things, making new creations that lead to old wisdoms, finding new awakening in ancient endeavours. Mark Townsend is such alchemy. Mark is both a Magician and Christian Priest, but don't let that frighten you away. Mark has the unusual drive to find the mysterious in Christianity and to combine both worlds to make a more universal spirituality. His work is unlike the common trend of modern clergy and Christian church. Mark envisions a personal spiritual evolvement with wonder, the miraculous as a natural part of daily life.

Mark speaks not from unrealistic thought, but by actual experience. His novel is formed from the magic of daily livingness and the shadows of life, with eyes to see behind the surface to the light within the dark depths. Mark's heroes are no saints, nor should they be. True heroes are often flawed so that we may see their struggles and know that we too can find an inner power to transcend our weaknesses into true strength. Do not expect overt preaching here. That is never the way of a Wizard. It surely is not the way of my students, even if they happen to be thought of as "preachers" by title.

Performing magic is meant to be artistic expression, even by the cheap trickster. At higher levels, magical performances are symbolic. "Use truth to show illusion and illusion to show truth" is one creed in our realms, as is my claim in performance "What I do is not real. It is not a fake. It is symbolic." Such phrases mean to suggest greater things, while bridging the uninitiated to their needs and expectations. Novels do this wondrously.

As my student, Mark Townsend performs and writes magic to suggest far greater depths. His use of symbol and story speaks to another part of us that listens attentively and expands while our conscious minds read surface ink on the page.

As you have come to this book in some way, there is something here for you. Wizards believe that coincidence is a base description, rather than an excuse. "Co-incidents" describe the situation, but hardly explain mysterious relationships away. The intent behind this book means that if you hold it, it has found you. Perhaps then you will find yourself within it. Something here is for you. That's why you hold it.

Wizards of the modern age still keep many ancient secrets and can hint only at what is within each of us. Wizards provoke students into a journey that leads within. Mark does this beautifully in his novel, and we shall both meet you as you travel there with us.

Never be fooled by those who insist that the basest view of life is the true view, or that your lack of outer experience overshadows what you know inside as your reality. No Wizard gives anything to you. We simply urge you onward to find your own truths – that which can be found within.

Between these covers is a beginning and ending. The end however is only a new beginning, as it always has been and will be always.

As we say in my School, we send you Many Blessings and Happy Successes Within and Without.

Kenton Knepper
March 2007

www.kentonmagic.com

PART 1

'SUNDAY'

CHAPTER 1

'Shit!'

He felt a sharp pain under his left ear and something wet on the skin of his shoulder. He looked down.

Blood?

Slowing his pace he lifted a hand to touch the wound. A small piece of twig jutted out from the skin. He pulled it free and continued pushing his way through the trees. No time to stop. No time to ponder. No time to have second thoughts.

At last he found the place and the old oak tree was just as he remembered. He climbed to a height of about twenty feet, sat on a branch and looked down. Just as required. No other branches directly below; a good clear drop! The ear had stopped bleeding, but his white shirt was now more like a butcher's apron. There were other cuts on his hands and one trouser leg was ripped at the knee. He didn't care. He was there for one purpose and worrying about his appearance was not it. There was now only one more thing to do, fasten the rope and tie the loop. He did it quickly and was ready.

The tortured man sat like a lynch mob victim waiting for the drop, the only difference being the mob was in his own mind. The pain from his ear was intense but nothing compared to the mental agony in his head.

It'll all soon be over. Eyes closed. Countdown. *Ten... nine... eight... seven... six... fi... f...* Silence! No number five!

The branch bowed and creaked, a leaf fell circling towards the ground and a squirrel from a neighbouring tree stopped gnawing an acorn to look. Overhead the sun shone, but no one would have known for the forest canopy was dense. A tiny silver thread unwound and brushed against his face, dropping off a passenger. The money spider crawled along his cheek but he didn't notice. He sat motionless, unexpected visions filling his mind. Moments later he awoke from the trance with a shudder, startling both the squirrel and the spider.

'My God,' he croaked, 'I can't do it.' His one hand clung on to the branch while the other loosened the rope that was wrapped round his neck. The slipknot moved an inch, then a little more, until finally the deadly necklace was free. Minutes later he stood at the base of the great tree gazing up at what might have so easily become his executioner. His vivid imagination had saved his life.

Still staring into the branches above he reached into a pocket and got out his mobile phone. He switched it on, took a deep breath, pressed a few buttons, and waited...

'Sam! Sam!' The voice was older than his, female and desperate.

'It's me,' he said.

'Oh Sam where are you?'

'I'm ok. I'm coming home.'

'Thank you God!' his mother whispered.

'I'm so sorry.' He hung up, slipped phone away and knelt down to wind up the rope. Half of his mind was fixed on home while the other half replayed the images he'd just seen when perched on the branch above. It had all happened in a matter of seconds, as though he was a sky TV freak flicking through the channels so quickly that the screen was a blur. The images that he *could* make out were confusing. Sam knew the notion that before you die your life flashes before you, but in his vision it was not *his life* that flashed before him, or at least not a life he had lived. *What could it mean?*

CHAPTER 2

Jane Weston sat at the table, cards spread out before her in an arc.

Damn I shouldn't be here.

To say she looked *a little* uncomfortable would be like saying a stalker's victim looked *a little* concerned. She would never have been seen in such a place were it not for her stupid promise.

Why the hell wasn't I stronger? What made me give in to her like that?

She'd let her guard down badly and she knew it. Caught crying in the works' WC is bad enough, but when it's by someone like Jenny Thrip? It seemed to Jane that the only conceivable way she was going to get away from the irritating self-appointed new age counsellor was to promise that she'd take her advice. But oh how Jane now wished she'd been more assertive as she sat facing the result of her bargain.

The room hummed with human muttering and the humidity caused by the vast number of attendees was suffocating. There was a haze, and accompanying smell, left by the many joss sticks on the various stalls. To Jane a psychic fayre was the last place on earth she'd choose to look for direction.

Only geeks and freaks come to these places, she thought to herself. *This'll be another complete waste of my time and money.* How wrong she was.

CHAPTER 3

Sam stepped through the door and fell into his mother's outstretched arms. For a while they just held each other without any words, simultaneously giving and receiving the comfort they both so desperately needed. They'd both been to hell and back. Yet if hell is a dark satanic pit into which people fall, both Sam and his mother were still standing close enough to the opening to taste the hot fiery sulphur of the devil's breath.

Eventually his mother spoke, 'My boy, what *possessed* you?' When folk use that term they usually don't mean what Sam's mother meant. 'This can't have come from *you!* People just don't drive off to the woods and...' she tried to say the words, but couldn't. 'They just don't, especially *people like us*.'

*

Sam Harper had grown up within the religious straight jacket of an ultra strict Christian fellowship. He *had* been the Deputy Head of their denominational school, and would have still been were it not for the divorce. The cold words of the Chief Governor, as he explained why Sam had to go, still haunted his vivid memory: 'Mr. Harper, we Christian educators must maintain our standards, especially *people like us*.'

*

People like us! Sam listened to the words again as his mind pressed the play back button in his head. How it hurt to hear the same phrase, spoken with the same half embarrassed tone, now coming from the mouth of his mother.

He loosened his grip and leant back, repositioning his hands on her shoulders. Sam looked his mother in the eyes. 'It's *people like us*, as you call them, who made *me* like *this*. I'm forty-three years old, divorced, jobless, pathetic and useless. All my damn life I've had *people like us* telling me what to think, what to believe, even who to marry. And where did it get me?' He took his hands away and slumped down in the armchair by his side.

CHAPTER 4

'Now dear, gather them up and mix them for me,' said the older woman.

*

Jane was in her early thirties and managed a cosmetic department within a large up-market city centre store. She always tied back her long dark hair so her customers could see the whole of her face. She oozed confidence.

'There you are. Now what?' she said.

'Good, deal out three cards face down.'

When she'd done so she looked up and saw the woman smiling at her and she felt it was genuine. Jane was surprised by her own reaction, for before it was too late to correct herself she'd smiled back. *Who is this person?*

'Ok when you are ready please turn a card over, any one of them.'

Jane looked at the three cards lying there before her. A few moments ago she'd wanted to run for it. Yet now she was intrigued. She studied the back of each card, and then settled on one – the middle one - reached out and turned it over. There she sat, card now facing her, eyes on stalks, transfixed and spellbound by the mystery that lay in front of her.

CHAPTER 5

Sam sat, head in hands. His mother was silent but he could feel her presence. His senses absorbed her waves of pity and revulsion like a sheet of slate absorbs the sun. All of a sudden his head rose like a robot whose power had just been turned on. His eyes were closed and his face was expressionless.

'Sam!' He could faintly hear her voice.

'Sam!' The voice was fainter.

'Ss...' Her mouth was moving and her eyes wide open and bulging, but all the sound had been switched. She knelt beside him and touched his hand. He didn't respond. He was rigid, motionless and immune to any inter-ference from the outside world. Yet inside his head he was running...

CHAPTER 6

'What is it my dear?'

Jane looked up at the psychic, 'you know don't you?' she said.

'The cards only show you what you already know.'

'But you know something! You know why I was so shocked when I saw *that*'. Jane went to touch the card with her finger but pointed instead.

'No. No I don't. I can't see what you are seeing, but I can help you to uncover what your inner voice is trying to tell you.'

'What are you, a clairvoyant or a shrink?'

'Neither,' said the woman, 'my role is that of a Reader. I know these cards and the messages they whisper. They speak because they resonate deeply with the human soul. They have no power of their own but connect with your inner self. They can be like signposts on an inner journey.'

'But I only came here today because I'd made a bloody stupid deal with a gossip!' Jane protested.

'On one level you are quite right. But can't you be open to the possibility that other forces are at work? I don't understand it either my dear, but it seems that sometimes the soul knows exactly what is required.'

Jane looked down at the table again. The card stared back at her.

*

Two months earlier Jane had been turned down for what would have been the opportunity of a life time and what made it harder to bear was the reason why. The job was to be the international ambassador for a new cosmetic chain called 'Visual Eloquence'. She'd been head hunted! She knew she'd got it. She had no doubt. So why did she let herself down so badly with her presentation? That question tormented her mind. Jane was an expert at such things, yet it had been a disaster. After only three minutes she'd managed to lose both the attention of the jury and the chance of a perfect career. Oh how she'd dreamed of it: a job that would take her to New York, Sidney, Moscow and Cape Town. But that's all she was left with – a dream.

*

The card continued to stare. It depicted a young woman in walking pose. The figure was sideways on and carrying a large back pack. Up above her head was the sun (on the left) and the moon (on the right). Even though she was clearly walking there was a large wall in front of her and on the wall a sign with minute writing on it. Across the top of the card were the words *The Traveller* and along the bottom *The physical journey denied, a spiritual journey implied.*

'What about the other cards?' said Jane.

'Well, my dear, I leave them in your hands. You've turned over the middle one and I can see it speaks of your present. If you feel ready to turn the other two then go ahead.'

Jane's hand trembled as she turned over the cards. At first they said nothing. Certainly no shocks or surprise like the first card. But after a while they began their subtle whispering…

CHAPTER 7

Sam was running, pushing himself through the trees. He was confused to find himself back in the forest, but this time it felt different. He was not desperate or depressed. He had no rope with him.

It didn't take him long to reach the oak tree. He stood underneath and looked up. He saw the branch and shuddered. Then he noticed something, a tiny fragment of white and red material stuck to the bark of the trunk.

Why am I here again? How did I get here?

'Do you really want to know?' The voice from behind shocked him. He spun round but saw no one.

'Who's there?' he said as a single bead of sweat trickled down his forehead. His heart pounded and his skin turned hot with panic. As far as Sam was aware he'd said nothing out loud.

'Sam,' the voice sounded familiar, 'you can't see me yet. You are dreaming, but you will see me when you awake. You have no need to fear me, and you will know where to find me. I have a gift for you, so come and seek me. It will all make sense in time.'

*

'Sam!' His eyelids fluttered.

'Oh Sam I was about to call an ambulance,' said his mother, 'what happened?'

He was still too dazed to speak.

'Sam, we have to see someone. I know, Revd. Morris. He'll know what to do.'

'Mmmm… Mo… th…er don't'

'What are you saying Sam?' She flipped through the phone book to the page marked M.

'No, pl… ease. I know wh… to do. Just… need some sleep now.'

'Alright,' she said, 'I won't call him until you've had a chance to rest.'

Mrs Harper helped her son up the stairs to his room and kissed him goodnight. She couldn't remember the last time she'd done that. She stood at the door gazing at him, a mixture of thoughts going through her mind, a mixture of feelings churning away in her stomach.

'God help him,' she sighed. Then added, 'And God help me too!'

CHAPTER 8

Three cards now faced the enchanted young woman. For a moment time stood still. She looked up at the reader, eyes full of tears.

'What is it?' said the older woman.

Jane just sniffed and looked back down at the table. A little pool of tears formed on the wooden surface.

'Here,' the woman handed Jane some tissues. 'For the table too,' she added.

Jane blew her nose, dabbed her eyes and wiped the table dry. Again she stared at the cards. To the left of the spread lay a mysterious looking card called *The Controller*. It portrayed a young man two thirds of the way up a long ladder which was propped up against a high window of a colossal tower. The ladder, tower and climber were so high that they reached the clouds. Higher still on the top right shone a few rays of sunlight like streaks of pure gold, and on the left was a flock of birds flying together into the sun. The man held one hand open and looked down at the ground. He had dropped something! He looked unsteady on the precariously high rungs of the ladder. On the ground lay a shattered clay jar with a pile of sparkling gold dust around it and along the lower edge of the card were the words *Perfection's futile dream; Through cracks true light will gleam.*

'What does it mean?' said Jane, wiping another tear from her cheek.

'I think you know,' said the reader.

'But you tell me you know these cards and their meanings,' Jane Protested.

'Yes my child, but every once in a while I meet someone who *knows*. I don't wish to frighten you but I feel that you will be able to read these cards for yourself.'

'For Christ's sake I don't even know if I buy any of this shit. I'm confused. I came here to get some bitch at work off my back, and now I've been dragged into all this voodoo crap.'

'Yet, my dear, even now inside your own mind you are arguing with yourself. A calmer, wiser self is talking isn't she?'

Jane knew the Reader was right. She'd been aware of that voice before. But now it was indeed talking.

Jane, don't fear. Don't resist. Listen to your self. Listen to me. Trust and be open and you will find the answers you didn't even know you were looking for. She shook her head as if she was ridding herself of water after a shower. Then she looked at the cards again.

The card to the right of the spread was the strangest of the three. Its title was *True Love* and it depicted a man and a woman looking each other across a pond. They had knives sticking into their backs yet were smiling and gazing across the rippling water with their arms stretched out towards each other. They stood apart with horrific wounds, yet wore no look of fear, or sorrow, or even longing - just contentment. The words at the bottom of this card were *Cling and you will kill, let go and you will keep. This is the purest love to seek.*

The Reader glanced at Jane and detected fascination but also tiredness. It had been a lot for her to take in. 'I feel we should draw this to a close for now,' said the reader, taking out a notebook and pencil. 'I want you to take these cards home with you. They no longer belong to me. Have my personal card too. You'll find there are various ways to contact me.'

'Have the cards? But…?'

'They are yours now my dear and they have so much more to say, more than a twenty minute sitting could ever achieve.'

Jane looked her in the eyes and saw compassion and honesty. 'What do I do with them?'

'Each morning take them out and lay them as they are now. Let them speak. Don't think too much. Just let your thoughts wander naturally. You will be shown many things, I assure you. In fact my dear, YOU will show you many things. And when you need to speak to me, you know how to get in contact.'

*

It turned out to be an exhausting day for Jane Weston and, being too tired to walk, she called a cab. The driver tried several times to chat but Jane didn't even hear him. She was in another place completely.

That night she slept deeply - *deeply* not peacefully. The images she'd been exposed to continued to haunt her mind as the hours of night passed by.

PART 2

'MONDAY'

CHAPTER 9

'*Mother!*'

'*Sam!*' She dropped the dish into the sink and dashed to the bottom of the stairs. She imagined herself throwing open his room and seeing him in a pool of blood with a razor in his hand, or even balanced on the window sill. But she'd misinterpreted his cry.

'Mother,' He was standing at the top of the stairs with a look of joy upon his face that she hadn't seen for years. His eyes were bright, his cheeks were rosy and his mouth, which had been a straight line for years, curved happily like a new moon on its side. His slouched body was now upright, and there was a spring in his limbs. The combination of his facial expression and his dancing pyjama clad body hinted of Mad King George.

'Sam, what's happened?'

'Mother dear, I know what to do.' For the first time in years he had hope! 'I know where I must go for the answers I'm looking for.'

'But Sam I've called Revd. Morris.'

His face darkened and his voice took on a new authority, 'No mother! I know what I'm going to do. You'll just have to trust me. I've been told.'

Mrs Harper looked at her watch. It was eight thirty. She remembered the Minister saying he'd call at around nine, straight after Morning Prayer with the elders. She wondered what Sam meant.

Where's he going? Will he take longer than half an hour to get ready? Can I beg him to wait and see the Minister first? What if I make him a cooked breakfast? Surely that would keep him till nine.

She looked up at him. His face was radiant again and for some reason she found herself saying the very words her mind was shouting at her not to say, 'Ok my son. You know what to do. I won't stand in your way. I promise you, but please just let me know where you are going.'

'Back to the forest,' he said as he disappeared back into his room for clothes.

*

Sam's father died when he was still just a boy. He often wondered whether this was the reason he'd got so attached to older men. He could remember various 'elders' from his past who he'd related to as father figures. There was Mr. Ginsburg his high school religious education teacher. In a somewhat severe educational environment, where the cane and slipper were dished out more regularly than the crap they served up for dinners, this kindly old tutor had always been warm and compassionate. Sam and four of his friends were once caught in the act of climbing on to the school roof by Mr. Ginsburg. They'd managed to find some crafty way of sneaking up there.

'Cum-eer you boys,' the old man bellowed, in a rather uncharacteristically aggressive manner. And down they all came, tails between legs. The usual punishment for such a crime was to be marched to the tutor's study and given a crisp whack on the backside. Four of them stood in an orderly line quaking like jelly while the first poor unfortunate was dragged into the room. Outside they could hear the sound of sobbing, then a swish through the air followed by a fleshy thud as the cane hit an arse.

'Next!' Ginsburg shouted, as the first tearful boy escaped.

Poor Sam was last in the queue and had to bear the added torment of hearing the torture of four of his fellow criminals.

At last it was his turn, 'Next!'

He entered the room and was asked to bend over an oak chair with a burgundy leather seat. 'Are you sorry?' said the teacher.

'Yes,' whimpered Sam.

'Will you do it again?'

'No'.

Whack! Sam waited for the pain, and then he twigged. *That old trickster!* Mr Ginsburg had taught those boys a lesson that day, but did not inflict pain to teach it. The clever old man called them in one at a time because he didn't want those outside to see how he was hitting not the boys' bums but the leather chair they were leaning against.

Sam grew very fond of Mr. Ginsburg. The two of them used to talk regularly about all sorts of things. He found he could be himself with the old man. For the last three years of his school life Sam felt like he had a father again.

There were others too - male mentors – who would appear at different stages of Sam's life. The last one had died at about the time of Sam's divorce.

*

Sam knew he'd find the tree without much difficulty, and there it was - tall, proud and arrogant, looking down at the human puppet on the ground. He pinched his face to make certain he wasn't dreaming. He wasn't!

Over the course of the last twenty four hours Sam had had three visions. Apart from the fact that it had saved his life the first one remained a mystery. All he remembered was that it seemed to be himself in the future. The second one, however, was vivid and real. He'd felt like he was really there. The voice was deep and familiar. But the vision that was taking present pride of place in Sam's mind, as he stood in that wood, was the one that had caused him to wake up that morning with such elation and excitement. Such was the intensity of the dream that he didn't even stop to consider whether his dashing off up the woods again was a reasonable reaction to a bed time imagination.

He looked around, but could see no one.

Where are you?

Crack! He spun round at the sound of a foot on a piece of brittle wood. Nothing! It happened again, the same sound. He peered in the direction of the noise as the deer stepped out from behind some bushes and, sensing Sam, skipped off into the woods.

Come on. You're supposed to be here? Sam's vision was vivid but now he was confused. The dream had been so convincing. He had met a man, an elderly man, near the old oak tree, and this man had answers. When he awoke he *knew* that he had to go back to the wood and look for this man. He didn't stop to ask himself how plausible this was, he just *knew*.

Please. Come on. You must be here.

'Hello,' he called, cupping his hands to make a cone.

After a whole hour of waiting and calling Sam's elation wore off. He felt let down. *Why am I such a sucker? Why do I let these bloody fantasies trick me?*

'And you', shouted Sam at God, 'why do you let me go through all this? Is this your sick revenge for a guy who proved to be too weak for your perfect club? Is this you getting back at me for my doubts? God I should have known that a vision about a strange teacher would have a catch. You wouldn't *really* have anything to teach me through a man in a wood. Your man's the Minister isn't it! You've led me up the garden path haven't you? Jesus I should have jumped.'

Sam slumped off back towards the car park, and as he walked he kicked and stamped and swore. He reached a place where the path split in two directions, one way to the car park and the other to a place called the Reading Chair. The walk calmed him slightly, but Sam couldn't bear the thought of going home to face his mother again so he decided to go and find this so-called Reading Chair. It wasn't far.

'All this bloody crap,' he muttered as he walked slowly up the narrow path towards what looked like some sort of wooden pagan monument. It was then that he noticed the old man sat on the odd looking chair. Sam wanted to turn round and walk away but suddenly, and without turning his head to look at Sam, the old man spoke.

'Odd looking thing isn't it?' he said.

Sam recognised the voice immediately.

CHAPTER 10

Jane sat at her breakfast table, with her three new cardboard companions laid out in front of her. It was now late morning. She'd woken feeling as though she hadn't slept, though she did not feel moody or low. Just shell shocked. As she sat there she remembered the Reader's words:

'Each morning take them out and lay them as they are now. Let them speak. Don't think too much. Just let your thoughts wander naturally. You will be shown many things, I assure you. In fact my dear, YOU will show you many things. And when you need to speak to me, you know how to get in contact.'

She looked down at the three strange images and smiled. *So, my friends, what are you going to tell me?*

CHAPTER 11

He was dressed in a well-worn pair of brown cord trousers and a shabby old green woollen coat, buttoned with two wooden toggles. There were other button holes, but the toggles had long since dropped off. He also wore a tatty hat that could have been picked up in a Middle Eastern bazaar.

'It's a Reading Chair,' said the old man, 'I come here often. I like the place. I find I can sit and think.'

Sam looked at him not knowing what to say. It was the voice he'd heard in his second vision.

'So what brings *you* here?' the old man inquired.

Sam didn't know how to answer him, 'I dunno, er… I'm looking for someone.'

'Do you mind me asking who?'

Sam looked down at the ground, and then up at the old man. The words were already travelling through the air before he could stop himself.

'Are you the Teacher? It's just your voice… it sounds…'

The old man smiled and looked directly into Sam's eyes, 'Why don't you sit down', he said. Sam obeyed.

For a while they sat in silence. Sam gazed out into the distance but saw nothing. Then the man spoke again, 'Teacher, you say?'

Sam's head turned and their eyes met. Sam noticed that the man had a short beard with a haphazard distribution of silver flecks scattered about in it. He also had two piercing yet honest amber coloured eyes. He was not a large man; no bigger than Sam himself (who was about five foot six) but he did carry a large presence. His face was clean, though well weather worn, and his long silver hair was tied back.

'Yes… er… no. Oh Look I'm sorry I'm so confused. I came up here this morning with a reason, a quest, but I've got it all so wrong. I'm sorry, look this isn't going to make any sense to you.' Sam got up. 'Sorry sir, I won't bother you any more.'

'Stop. Wait!'

Sam walked back down the path.

'Stop.'

The young man was determined.

'Please stop *Sam*.' Said the old man.

Sam span round a stared at the man. 'How the hell do you know my name?' he demanded.

'You're wearing it,' replied the old man.

Sam looked confused but then he remembered and grabbed at his neck. Sure enough his chain had come out from where he normally wore it under his shirt, and from the chain dangled his baptismal pendant. It was a large silver circle with words of scripture engraved around the rim and his own name SAM in the centre.

'I see,' said Sam.

'I figured it was your name,' said the man, 'because I've come across these before. In fact I used to have one myself, but lost it many years ago.'

'You belonged to the same fellowship as me?'

'It seems I did.'

Sam began to feel himself relax. He walked back over to the Reading Chair and sat down again. The two men faced each other and the younger one began to talk while the older one listened and listened.

CHAPTER 12

Jane decided to take one card at a time. She began with the one on the far left of the spread, picking it up, holding it close to her eyes and then returning it to its place on the table. She gazed down repeating quietly the words of the Reader, 'Each morning take them out and lay them as they are now. Let them speak. Don't think too much. Just let your thoughts wander naturally. You will be shown many things, I assure you. In fact my dear, YOU will show you many things.'

'Speak then,' she said, staring hard at *The Controller.* She let her eyes work their way over every square centimetre of the card taking in each detail, the climber, the tower, the sunlight, the pot, the clouds and the birds. She read again the words at the bottom, *Perfection's futile dream; Through cracks true light will gleam.* She noted the position of the young man on the ladder. He was quite close to the top and therefore almost ready to step across onto the tower, yet he also looked so unstable, so fragile.

Why's he dropped the clay pot? And what's all that gold stuff scattered down the ladder and in a heap on the floor?

Jane had so many questions. Then she noticed something else, up in the far left corner of the picture. At first she wondered how she'd missed it. A bird was flying in the *wrong* direction. Now she could see it plain as daylight. A flock of birds were flying into the sun in unison, all apart from one bird who was clearly flying in the opposite direction.

How strange. Surely birds don't do that? So why would this one fly backwards?

She moved her head closer to the card. *Come on little fellow! Tell me why you are flying that way?*

It was as if the answer just appeared in her head. She suddenly knew why the bird was acting that way. Was it pure intuition? Was it divine inspiration? Was it her deeper wiser self talking? She didn't know. All she did know was the answer to her question.

The bird flies away from danger. The bird sees something the others cannot see, and the danger is the sunlight.

Jane chuckled and looked around herself. She knew no one else was in the house but she felt almost embarrassed by her excitement. She looked again at the card and as if to confirm her interpretation noticed something else she'd missed. There it lay, on the very top of the tower, the tiny speck of a dead bird.

So if the sunlight is so dangerous, why is the man also climbing towards it?

Brrrrrrrrrring! The door bell startled Jane, and the last thing she needed right now was an intruder. She looked at her watch. *Ten past twelve! Who could that be?* She forced herself up, made her way to the front door, and opened it.

'Hi Jane!' said Jenny Thrip.

CHAPTER 13

'That's quite a story,' said the old man, looking at Sam with penetrating eyes.

'Do you believe me?'

'Sam, yes I believe you, the mind is a powerful tool. On the one hand it can lead us to fantastic, life changing discoveries, or on the other hand drag us down into the darkest pits of despair. Yes Sam I believe everything you've told me, and maybe together we can find the answers to your visions?'

'Are you offering to help me? But you don't even know me, and I don't know you.'

'Sam, do you believe in magic?'

'What?'

'Do you believe in *magic*?'

The question threw him completely. His mind went into overdrive. *What the hell's he doing talking about magic? Who is this man? I thought you were guiding me God. He doesn't fit in with your ways. What am I doing here?*

Sam looked at the man, shuddered and breathed in deeply. *Magic? What kind of a question is that? Why would God lead me with these visions? Why would he...?* Sam's eyes suddenly opened wide as though he'd been shocked. Then the colour started to run from his face. *No! it can't be! It mustn't be.* The truth slowly dawned. *Not the devil?* Sam was looking at the old man.

'Are you still a believer?' asked Sam.

'A believer?'

'Yes, you said you had a pendant like mine, which means you've been baptised into the fellowship. Are you still a believer?'

'Sam, if you are asking me do I still believe in God, then the answer is yes, but do I believe in the institutions that try to follow this God? Sam, I'm afraid that kind of belief left me many years ago.'

'Then you can't help me. I've got it all wrong.'

'Sam, I also came here to meet someone today. I thought I had met him. Perhaps I too was wrong.'

Sam looked at the old man. He could see honesty and tenderness in his deep amber eyes. The young man looked away, then turned his whole body and walked.

CHAPTER 14

That bloody nosey cow!

Jane finally closed the door on her unwelcome visitor.

Trust her to ask where I was and trust work to tell her.

She was now too agitated to go back to the cards. All she could do was jot down a few notes on what she'd discovered so far. She finished writing and put the note book next to the cards on the table. Then she decided on a treat, a luxury she'd denied herself for years… to make a pot of fresh coffee, blow the dust off a favourite old video film and slump in front of the TV for a few hours.

The videos were stored in a cardboard box under the stairs. Jane opened the box and tipped out some films. It didn't take her long to decide… there in the midst of the pile was a movie she used to watch with her brother and sister as children. Just seeing the cover brought deep feelings of nostalgia. *That's the one.* Without even knowing it, synchronicity was working and Jane's luxurious treat of cinematography and coffee was about to take her even deeper into her journey of self discovery.

CHAPTER 15

Sam slammed the door and stomped into the living room throwing himself down onto the sofa. His eyes stared at the TV screen, which was turned off, and he breathed heavy breaths through his nose like a penned up bull itching to be let loose on the matador. He didn't notice his mother as she appeared in the doorway.

'Sam, what happened?'

He chose not to turn his head. His eyes remained on the imaginary dot at the centre of the screen.

'I'm going mad,' he whispered.

'Sam, I've spoken to the Minister and he wants to see you… as soon as possible. He told me to call him when you came back. Can I now? Will you at least listen to what he has to say my son?'

Sam didn't care anymore. He was exhausted by his lows, highs and even deeper lows. He felt picked up and put down and totally confused. He sat there wishing he'd ignored the first vision and just dropped.

'Do whatever you want,' he said, 'I'm not going anywhere now.' The only consolation of his mood was that he didn't feel frightened at the prospect of meeting the Minister.

Revd. Bloody Morris, he thought to himself, *whose dammed fellowship has been the bane of my life. Why do I still let them have control over me?* He thought again of the green-clothed man and wondered why it was that his church leader scared him so much whereas this old man had been so unintimidating. *Can he be so bad? Can he be dangerous just because he doesn't believe anymore? But magic! Oh God why does it always have to be so damn confusing?* Sam's questions added to his tiredness.

*

'Hello Sam,' The Minister stood over him as he twitched and forced open his eyes. His unanswerable questions had coaxed him to sleep, like the counting of sheep.

'I'm sorry,' Sam sat up rubbing his face and blinking, 'I must have dropped off.'

'Don't get up,' said Revd. Morris, 'I'll sit down. Your mother's making us some coffee.'

'I'm sorry,' said Sam, looking at the floor, 'It's just been horrible lately, and…'

'Lately?' The Minister didn't let Sam finish.

'What do you mean by that?' Sam's voice changed from apologetic to defensive.

'I mean, Sam, that you haven't been a regular worshipper since your problems, and how many years is that? It's no wonder you've had such a traumatic time. Sam you need the fellowship around you. You need our support, our protection, our prayers, our lo…'

'Don't you dare! Don't say that word. You think you demonstrated *love* when you stopped me taking the bread and wine? And what *love* did you show to Susan? Ok she left the fellowship, but why the hatchet job Revd. Morris? Why couldn't you just let her leave with grace?'

Sam looked again at the non existent TV picture and saw an image that he'd tried to forget. An evening meeting on a hot summer's day. The fellowship gathered together to hear the verdict on one of their member couples' fate. The couple had decided to part in an amicable manner. She, Susan, had grown apart from the fellowship as well as from her husband. She, like her husband, was a cradle member and needed to break free. She'd come to the point of spiritual and emotional suffocation. Added to that was the tension over children. Sam had always wanted them but Susan felt unready. In the Minister's opinion it was her duty to have children and she was therefore failing as a wife and as a Child of God. She'd had enough of it but divorce in such circumstances was out of the question in the eyes of the fellowship. However she'd stuck to her guns and begun proceedings. The Elders had met and discussed the situation and now the whole church had been called together to be told the will of God. Sam was there but Susan couldn't face it. She would have to wait to hear the verdict second-hand.

Sam watched the imaginary scene unfold in his mind and listened again to the Minister's chilling words: 'Mr Harper, you have allowed what is sacred to be broken. As a constant reminder of your disunity you will no longer receive the sign of unity, the bread of Our Lord. Until your marriage is restored you will be welcome only as a half brother. As for Mrs Harper, who has become an apostate, she should not be engaged in conversation with any member until full and true repentance has been made.'

Sam remembered the scene vividly, and grimaced with revulsion. But his grimace was not just at the memory of those repulsive official words but at the memory of his own weak and pathetic willingness to go along with it all. *Not any more.*

'She was a traitor,' said the proud churchman.

'Not half the traitor you are, you self righteous bully.'

'Sam!' His mother screamed from the hall and ran into the room carrying a tray of coffee but spilling some of it on the floor in the process.

'What mother? Am I out of order? Am I embarrassing you?'

'Sam,' the Minister's voice was calm and quiet, 'Dear Sam, let's not argue, we're brothers'

'Half brothers!'

The Minister ignored him and continued, 'Look, let's agree on a plan. You know you need to talk, and I need to say some things. Why don't you talk, for as long as you need, and I promise to listen without interrupting. Then I will talk while you listen? What do you think?'

Sam looked at the Minister. Then he looked at his mother. Then he looked back at the blank screen. 'Ok,'

Revd. Morris asked Sam's mother to leave them and for the second time that day Sam went through the whole story, going over every detail of all three visions and the meeting with the old man. The Minister kept his promise and listened.

*

'Have you finished?' asked Revd. Morris after Sam had finally stopped talking.

'I have,' said Sam.

CHAPTER 16

Music played, marking the end of the film and Jane watched the titles scroll upwards and disappear into the top of the screen. For the last one and a half hours she'd been in a trance, her imagination held captive by the four characters' search for the mysterious Wizard. Now, back to reality, she heard the sound of her tummy rumbling and glanced at her watch. *2pm? Gosh no wonder I'm hungry.* She lent forward, pointed the remote at the screen and clicked it off.

Her tummy made noises again. Half of her wanted to get up and head for the kitchen while the other half wanted to go back into the trance. She sat with her head tilted back resting on a cushion, her mind filled with images that she hadn't seen for such a long time – familiar images yet now speaking to her in a whole new way. She decided it was too important to forget. The food would have to wait. She got up and walked over to the table with the notebook and cards, sat down, picked up her pen and, under the notes she'd previously made about the cards wrote:

I don't know what's happening but I know I need to write. I'm not even sure who I'm writing this for. I feel confused but excited. I've just watched a film that I've seen so many times. As a child I saw it every Christmas without fail, yet today it was not just a film, and not just a walk down memory lane. It rang bells... huge loud bells. A girl who finds herself on a journey she's not asked for; a girl who is given three strange new friends to travel with and learn from. A journey to find a powerful wizard who himself turns out to be a frail man. Four co-travellers with four individual quests, each of them discovering that the very thing they thought they needed they actually possessed all along.

Am I Dorothy? I feel like I've been placed at the beginning of a yellow brick road. Was I meant to go to that psychic fayre? Was I even meant to screw up my presentation? I have so many questions. Why am

I so excited by all this? I've never been into this kind of thing, not since my early teens. And what about the cards and the things I wrote only a couple of hours ago? Have I been caught up in some delusion or was that Reader-woman for real? Are the cards she gave me really going to take me on a journey?

Jane re-read what she'd written and then turned back a page to glance over her earlier notes:

Card number 1 - The Controller. Perfection's futile dream; Through cracks true light will gleam.

A young man climbing a huge ladder, propped up against a tower. He is close to the top and looks unstable and fragile. There is a flock of birds but one bird is flying in the wrong direction. A dead bird lies on top of the tower. I think that the dead bird has been killed by the sun and the other bird is flying away from the sun. The man is climbing toward it/into it. It seems he has dropped a pot of gold dust. There is a small pile of yellow gold powder next to the broken pot as well as a scattering of it all down the rungs of the ladder.

Those last words leapt from the page, *gold dust!* In an instant she'd reached over and grabbed the cards. Jane held *The Controller* in her hand and tried to keep herself calm as she stared trembling at the yellow ladder.

Yellow ladder! *Yellow* brick road! Oh God!

CHAPTER 17

Revd. Morris took a large gulp of coffee and placed his cup and saucer back onto the little table by his side. He looked at Sam and smiled.

'Sam, you are not going to find this easy... but... I think you are under serious attack, spiritual attack!'

Sam opened his mouth as if he was going to speak, but the Minster saw it coming. 'Sam, you gave me your word, and I kept mine. Just let me say what I have to say.' He continued, 'I think a combination of things have led to this. Clearly the saga with Susan was the catalyst, but if you'd have trusted us, and stayed close to the fellowship, you'd have been kept safe under our protection. As it happened you chose to succumb to your own anger and pride and your soul became an open door for all the forces that would want to take control.'

Sam sat still, looking at nothing, chewing the inside of his mouth. Meanwhile the Minister talked on explaining all the points at which if only Sam had have acted differently this terrible depression would not have afflicted him so greatly. He took out his small black leather bound bible and quoted passage after passage until Sam's head was spinning. Yet even within all the turmoil and confusion Sam noticed something that was too obvious to miss. This Minister, with all his words of God and salvation, showed not one glimmer of love or compassion towards him. It was made more obvious because the last person he had spoken with (apart from his mother) was the old man and, though Sam had been highly unnerved by him, he had also found him warm and concerned.

The Minister finished. His words of wisdom and warning were complete. Now it was up to Sam. He'd been shown the way and the ball was in his court. He could continue in his rebellious journey of following demonic visions and potentially selling his very soul or he could repent, receive a spiritual cleansing, and come back to the fellowship. The Minister had even thrown in a little spiritual carrot: if Sam chose the latter he would be made a full member again.

CHAPTER 18

'Hello!'

'Is that…er!' Jane realised she didn't even know her name. 'Is that the… Reader?'

'Yes Jane, I thought you'd ring today.'

'Please, is there any chance of seeing you? I have so many questions. I know it's only been a day but…'

'Of course my dear. You can come to me at my home if you like. I'm free tomorrow morning. Can you make it then?'

'Yes, I'll have to make up another excuse for work but yes, thank you. How do I get there?'

The Reader explained the route but added, 'Take your mobile and ring me when you get close. The house is a little hard to find so I'll direct you for the final few yards which you can do on foot. Let's aim for about 10am.'

CHAPTER 19

Sam Harper was a good looking man in his early forties and, for a fellowship member, surprisingly well dressed. The only time this slipped was immediately following the divorce when looking good was his last concern. His hair was brown and cropped short, and he had honest eyes. However those very eyes were now red and staring down at the floor.

He remained silent but in his mind he spoke through gritted teeth. *How dare he? He thinks he's got me like a fish on a hook! He has no right to say those things about Susan. He has no right to bully people like this. He's tried to control my life for too long...*

But Sam's inner voice was not totally unified. It was as if he was arguing within himself. ***Sam! Don't be crazy. You are in the wrong. Don't forget it was you who've neglected your spiritual life.***

Shut up! Shut up! I can't stand this anymore. This is why I was up that bloody tree.

No Sam. Don't blame your turmoil on the fellowship. You were up that tree because you've lost your faith and hope. You never used to be like this. Come on, you never used to swear or drink like you do. You are out of control.

Please stop. Please God tell me what to do. Do I let this man talk me into his church again? God, are you part of this?

No Sam God is not a part of this. In fact because you are so deep in sin and following your own path He can't even see or hear you right now. The visions you've been having are from the other place. God can't look upon darkness Sam.

The poor man's conflicting thoughts were making him mad. He looked up at Rev.d Morris who was smiling. All of a sudden the cheesy expression vanished!

'Screw you!' said Sam to the Minister, *and Screw you too* said one of his inner voices to the other. 'I was going to kill myself yesterday, and if I did I'd have been thrown into hell itself. That's what *you* teach. Well something stopped me didn't it? And the something that stopped me was a vision. It was a vision of my future. I have a future you see. And I'm going to pursue it. Don't tell me God was not part of that. Why would the devil have stopped me killing myself when it would have been a ticket into *his* world?'

His thoughts came fast now, and his head suddenly cleared. 'I've allowed myself to be bullied by you for too long. The time's come for me to take a risk. I'm going to find the old man, the Teacher. I'm going to find him because he has something for me.'

He walked out of the room leaving the Minster in a state of shock. His mother, who'd heard it all, was in the hall looking stunned. She'd never seen her son like that before.

'I'm going for a walk mother. When I come back I'll expect the Minister to be gone. Tomorrow morning I'm going back to the woods.'

PART 3

'TUESDAY'

CHAPTER 21

Sam gulped down his last spoonful of corn flakes and, while still eating, got up and grabbed his coat. He opened the front door and walked across to the car that was parked by the roadside. Suddenly he noticed something in the corner of his eye and spun round.

'*Oomph!*'

The woman walked straight into him. She'd been talking on a mobile and not paying full attention.

'I'm sorry,' she said looking concerned.

'Don't worry,' he replied with a strained voice and grimacing.

'Oh shit I've hurt you!'

'No… please… I'm just a little winded.' Sam smiled as he spoke. 'It's no problem… honestly.'

The woman still looked concerned. 'Ok,' she said, 'as long as you're alright'. She was still holding the mobile and the voice on the other end was faintly audible, *'What's happening? Is everything ok my dear?'*

'You'd better go,' said Sam, acknowledging the mobile and voice.

'Ok… look I'm really sorry,' said the woman.

'I know. It's ok. I promise,' said Sam, as he opened the car door to get in.

Sam drove, and as he drove, so he thought, and as he thought so his mind began to chatter again. He felt surprisingly calm, the only discomfort being the fading ache caused by the woman's collision. The authority he'd taken over the Minister had given him a feeling of inner strength and a sense of self-respect, both of which were new. And though his more critical and punishing inner voice was always ready to lash out it was very much quieter this morning.

Ok let me think. What am I going to say? Do I apologise for yesterday and explain why I was unnerved? Or do I stand my ground and question him?

He probably won't even be there you fool?

He will be. I don't know why but I just feel he will be. Yesterday can't have been a coincidence. My dreams can't all be wrong. Something's happening... I can feel it.

The thoughts continued all the way to the forest car park. Sam climbed out of the car and opened the back door for his boots. He also grabbed the pen and note pad that he kept in the glove compartment. *Just in case,* he thought.

The Reading Chair was easy to find, even though he'd only been there once before. He found the sign and correct path and quietly made his way.

Suddenly he heard a voice calling from behind, 'Sam'.

He knew at once who it was and spun round. The old man was walking hurriedly, pushing himself along with a shepherd's staff.

'Sam, I'm so glad you came back. We've got much to talk about. Come on – follow me.'

Sam watched the man walk past and turn his head to beckon him to follow.

Sa...

Shut up. He didn't allow his critical voice any room to speak. *I'm going to follow him. I don't know where he's taking me or what he's going to show me, but I'm going. For once in my life I am going to follow my own instincts.*

The old man allowed Sam to catch up and turned to face him.

'Sam I know you are still feeling apprehensive. Please trust me, and if you can't trust me at least trust in your God. Everything will become clear, I promise.'

Even though it was only yesterday that Sam had fled from the same wood, today he felt content. Something inside him made him feel more secure. They walked side by side in the direction of the Reading Chair.

'Who are you?' asked Sam.

'Sam, the question you should ask is not who am I but *why* am I?

'What do you mean?'

'Again I promise you it *will* all make sense and you *will* know who I am but for now I think a better question for you is *why* I am here?'

'Ok, why are you here?' They approached the path to the Chair and Sam could see it in the distance.

'There it is,' said the old man, 'Let's go and sit down.'

They approached the Chair and the old man carefully placed his stick against it and sat down. Sam positioned himself next to him and looked around at the strange monument.

'What are *they*?' he asked, pointing up at the odd looking carvings on the under side of the roof.

'They're Runes,' said the old man, 'an ancient Nordic alphabet, and a favourite divinatory tool for mystics.'

'Divination! People tell fortunes with them?' said Sam with a sceptical tone.

'Some do, yes. But they are so much more than that. Right now, however, that's not what we're here to discuss. The most important question for you to consider is why I am here. In fact why are we both here?'

'And *why are we*?'

'Sam I am here because you called me.'

I don't understand.'

'Nor do *I* fully, but when I saw you yesterday I knew that you were the one I had been asked to help. Sam you're not the only person here who's had dreams and visions lately. Exactly one week ago I began having restless nights. I dreamed of this Reading Chair, a place I come often. But in my dreams I saw myself with another man, a younger man - a man who needed help. I kept a log of my dreams. For five nights we met and spoke and each night we discussed a different concern. Then on the sixth night there was no meeting, no discussion and no dream of a younger man. I woke that morning *knowing* I had to come here. That's when I met you.'

'This is so hard for me to take in,' said Sam. He was aware of how weird it all sounded and how his Minister and mother would be screaming *'leave that place, he's a devil, get away from him,'* but Sam also felt a strange inner warmth and excitement as the old man spoke. He'd experienced this feeling before when, as a child, he used to believe he'd heard God's voice. He once mentioned it to his mother who responded by dragging him before the Elders for being so presumptuous. They told him to beware inner voices, 'everything should be tested against Scripture and the teaching of the fellowship', they warned.

The old man continued, 'Sam I know you've been through hell. I know life's been tremendously hard for you. When you told me your story yesterday I felt for you. I could also see your confusion and fear when I asked you if you believed in magic.'

Sam's eyes widened a little. The word still had such connotations for him. 'Yes, in my fellowship we were always told to avoid magicians, wizards, witches and the like.'

'Sam I use the word to describe the unexplainable and wonderful ways of nature... super nature really. Magic is all around us. In your fellowship you are used to saying God's spirit is all around. I'm just using a different term for the same thing.'

'But God's not a magician.'

'No? But surely the fact that He somehow created this wonderful universe and caused everything to come into existence out of nothing, and that He formed you and I, and that right now we are sat here talking this way is rather magical don't you think?'

Sam couldn't argue. 'So you *do* believe He was behind my visions that brought me here to you?'

'Yes Sam I do. And I also believe He has given me five gifts to pass on to you'

'Pardon?'

'Sam, each of those five nights of dreams was a discussion between me and a younger man. On the sixth night I knew I had to come here. Last night – the seventh night - I had another dream. It was the most vivid and by this morning I knew I had to meet *you* for five days. Sam will you come here five more times beginning tomorrow? I have something to give you each day… five gifts that will be of great value as you continue your way in this confusing world.'

Sam's instincts told him to trust. He was fascinated and wanted to ask more. 'Who are you?' he asked.

'I told you before, that's not the important question. But let me ask you, who do you think I am?'

Sam tried to hold back on vocalising what was in his mind but it came out before he could stop himself. 'You're a Wizard.' He said.

'Then let that be who I am for you, the Wizard. In mythology the Wizard is the keeper of ancient wisdom. I hope to share such wisdom with you Sam.'

For a while the two men sat in silence. The older one took a deep breath and took in the various aromas of the wood. 'mmmmmmmh,' he sighed. The younger one, however, remained silent yet his mind began to talk.

Wizard? What do think you're doing you fool?

But he seems so genuine. I trust him. I know I should be wary but I do trust him.

You should leave now and go and see Revd. Morris. He'll help you.

NO! No I refuse to listen to you now. You always fill me with doubts and fear. Fear's not from God. This man does not scare me. I'm going to take him up on his offer. I'm going to meet him for the next five days.

*

Sam had always been plagued by an over active imagination and, though he usually referred to it as his curse, he also knew it could be a blessing. From a young age he'd create scenarios in his mind. He would see things. One time he was invited on a school trip to France and in those days the only way to cross the channel was a ferry-boat. He was eight years old. It was about two weeks before the event when he started having nightmares about being drowned. He told his mother and she said 'don't be silly, you're a child of God. He won't let anything happen.' But Sam didn't buy it. Not only was his imagination vivid his mind never stopped questioning and analysing… even at this young age. His memory even flashed back to a TV report of when a whole group of children had been in a coach accident. Five of them had lost their lives and seventeen were seriously injured. He figured that at least some of them must have been 'children of God'.

The days went by and he tried to muster up the courage to confront his mother again. He eventually managed but it was no use. So, when the day finally came Sam went missing. His mother was furious but there was nothing she could do. He'd gone. The trip went ahead without him and all the other children had a marvellous time with no accidents.

Look what you missed, he said to himself, as he saw all the delighted children on their first day back to school grinning with glee.

*

The Wizard finally spoke. 'Sam I'm going to leave you now. I think you need the rest of this day to come to terms with what I've said and decide whether you can trust me.' He pointed to a tree smothered with dark green ivy. 'At the moment your life is a little like that but the weeds that smother your life are not exterior but interior. Today I want you to go for a long walk – here in this forest – and listen to your quieter voice. There is wisdom in that voice. I KNOW you know what I mean. The other voice will try to confuse you.'

'How do know about my voices?'

'Sam we all have them, I've just learned how to listen to the right one. You, along with most other people, still allow the voice of confusion too much reign. Here's a thought that might help you. Whenever the voice feels like that ivy, twisting and pulling and suffocating your thoughts, then it is probably not your friend. The voice to listen to is the voice that is quieter, calmer, un-flustered and unconfused.'

'Yes I *do* know that voice.'

'Good, then spend today walking, listening, and enjoying being here. Did you bring any money?'

Sam suddenly looked concerned. 'Yes,' he said, 'why?'

'You'll need to eat,' said the Wizard with an emphatic smile, 'Use the little café near the car park. It's important to get some lunch. I want you to feel comfortable and content.'

'Ok,' said Sam, 'I'll spend the day here and do what you say. And then what?'

'Then if you feel you want to go ahead we'll meet tomorrow at around 10am. Come to this spot and I'll have ready the first of your five gifts.'

Sam felt a whole cloud of butterflies fly through his stomach. It was a pleasant anticipatory feeling, reminiscent of the feelings he once had lying in bed on Christmas Eve. He turned and looked into the old man's face. His eyes seemed to glow. Their deep amber colour fascinated Sam. He'd never seen eyes like that before. Interestingly his own eyes had always been described as amber, but they never sparkled and glistened like the Wizard's.

'There's something about you,' said Sam, 'something familiar.'

'It will all be made clear Sam. If you do decide to come back (and I hope you do) then by the end of this week those suffocating strands of ivy will be able to poison your thoughts no more.'

'Do you think there's a chance I might *not* come back?'

'Yes there is a chance. A voice inside you is now more fearful than ever, because it knows its power is being threatened. It will try everything, but because you are now aware of this it will be a harder task for your other voice has been given new strength.'

Sam got up and held out his hand. The Wizard, still seated, raised his and the two men shook hands.

'I *will* see you tomorrow,' said Sam.

'I do hope so,' said the Wizard.

With that Sam turned and walked back down the path towards the car park. He paused at the sign posts and wondered which of the many routes to take. In a flash a thought entered his mind. He *knew* exactly where to go.

CHAPTER 22

Jane had laughed, cried, reminisced, regretted, imagined and sat in spell-bound wonder all morning.

'I can't believe this,' she said. 'It's just so not me, all this psycho-spiritual stuff.'

The two women had looked again at the cards and, with the Reader's guidance, Jane now felt she'd understood a little more of their language. The older woman left Jane at the table with her journal. She'd instructed her to jot down everything that came into her mind while she would go and make a bite to eat for lunch.

My three cards. (left) The Controller, (centre) The Traveller, (right) True Love

First card turned - centre = the present. Subtext - The physical journey denied, a spiritual journey implied.

My notes: When plans to move are shattered a deeper force may be at work and more subtle inner movements of the soul may be taking place.

Lesson: Surrender to what is, and look for signs of growth, spiritual and emotional development.

Personal application: For whatever reason I was denied my dream of physical travel, but have been given an opportunity for a new spiritual and psychological journey. WOW.

Second card turned – left = The past / the character formed. The ego.

Subtext - Perfection's futile dream; Through cracks true light will gleam.

My notes: The hardest card to fully interpret. Much symbolism and detail. I see myself on that ladder, straining to climb and carrying the trophies of my success. Yet I also see that these trophies somehow need letting go of for their true glory to be revealed . . . the gold dust spilling out from the broken pot.

I know I am a perfectionist and an achiever in every area of my life from work to relationships. The card seems to warn that such ambitious lifestyles can potentially lead to death – the dead bird frazzled by the hot sun.

The gold dust also paves the way for a journey... but it is a journey DOWN the ladder not UP higher. The truth is at the bottom. What truth is this?

Still much interpretation needed here... my thoughts continue.

Jane stopped writing as the Reader called her into the kitchen for some lunch.

CHAPTER 23

Sam stood beneath the great oak tree again. He knew he needed to be there. It seemed strange looking up at the branch where he had sat with the rope round his neck. He decided to climb again and, within a few minutes, was sat back on the branch. As he sat and thought he became aware of words entering his mind. They were words that needed vocalising and, when he opened his mouth, he discovered they were a prayer:

'My Lord, my God, I've been so stupid these last few years. I've drifted so far from you. I'm sorry for all the turmoil I've caused. I wanted to die last time I sat here. I wanted to end everything. But now I have hope, yet I can't claim I'm not confused. My God I trust this man, this... Wizard. It seems so far from what the fellowship would endorse but I trust him. Please help me to see if it's a wrong turn. Help me to know one way or the other. Amen.'

Sam stayed there for quite some time. He tried to remember the pictures and images he saw when he was about to jump but nothing came. He climbed down and set off to find the café and, after his early lunch, went back to the same spot again. It brought him a strange sense of comfort. He had no idea what the week ahead was going to bring and was understandably unsettled, but being at the place where the first vision saved him gave him a great feeling of connectedness. He was in the middle of an unfolding plan.

*

On the way home that afternoon Sam sat behind the steering wheel wondering what tomorrow would bring. So far his critical mind had been quiet but he was cautious not to let his guard down. He drove down the hill from the woods and past the garage at the bottom. He could see a couple of guys chatting as one of them pumped petrol into a white van. He drove on and noticed some cattle standing in a huge field nibbling at the grass. Then, on a little further, he drove past the golf course and caught the flash of a man taking a swing.

What's happening to me, he thought to himself, *I never usually notice these things?*

Sam had been a dreamer all his life. He could walk into a cinema full of friends and not notice one of them. He sometimes looked as though he were in a trance. Yet driving his car home from the woods he noticed things he'd normally miss - ordinary things, everyday things, mundane things that people take for granted.

He pulled up outside his house and locked the car door. Then he saw something that, even in his dreamy state, he could not have missed. Propped up again the door to the house was a bouquet of flowers.

Wonder who they're for.

He walked over and stooped down to pluck off the little card. The envelope had no recipient's name but simply said 'an apology for the bruise.' Sam immediately remembered the incident in the morning. He tore apart the envelope, opened the card and read it: 'I didn't catch your name but please accept these as a sign of my apology. Jane!'

No number or address! Damn. She was lovely.

He clicked open the front door and crept in carrying the flowers.

'Mother,' called Sam.

There was no response. *I guess she's at some fellowship do.*

Sam grabbed a vase, filled it with water and arranged the flowers to the best of his ability. As he did so his mind conjured up images of the woman who had sent them to him.

Pretty girl Sam. Better go and look for her tomorrow hey. You can't let this happen and not do anything about it.

CHAPTER 24

It was evening and Jane had had a long day. Now she slept, and her dreams were full. Her sleep brought her intermingled images of card symbolism, Jenny Thrip, the Reader, wizards and yellow roads, and the man whose name she didn't know. Her alarm was set for 7.30am. Tomorrow she would go back to work.

PART 4

'WEDNESDAY'

CHAPTER 25

'Sam, are you there?'

His mother's voice dragged him out of his dream.

'Sam?'

'Yes… mother,' he shouted back, 'what?'

'Someone's at the door for you,'

He looked at his watch. *8am! Who on earth could want me at this time?*

Reluctantly he climbed out of bed and went to click off the alarm that had been set for 8am. It just began ringing at he pressed his hand down to quell the noise. *Oh well at least I was going to get up at this time.*

'I'm on my way' he shouted, as he pulled on his trousers.

Sam squeezed on a sweatshirt and made his way to the top of the staircase. There at the bottom, standing on the inside of the front door next to his mother, was a young woman.

'I'm so sorry for getting you up,' she said, 'I just wanted to give you this before I went off to work'. She watched him walk slowly down the stairs and held out a small rectangular card. Sam reached the bottom step and took it.

'Your business card?' he said. His mother looked at them both and walked into the kitchen.

'Yes, I didn't have one on me yesterday, and it was too late to drive home for one. I would have put one in with the card and flowers, just to let you know who it was who sent them. Are you ok?'

'Me? Oh yes. I'm fine. Honestly, it was nothing. You really didn't need to…' Sam stopped himself… 'But thank you. The flowers were lovely. It was kind of you.'

'What's your name?'

'Sam, Sam Harper… and yours is Jane…' Sam looked at the business card for her surname. 'Ah, Jane Weston - pleased to meet you Jane,' he said, as he held out his hand.

As Sam took her right hand in his he also noticed her left hand. There was a small gold signet ring on her little finger but no sign of any others.

'And I'm pleased to meet *you* Sam. Anyway I must get off to work. I haven't been in for a few days so I'm going early today. Say thank you to your mother won't you.'

'I'm here dear,' said Sam's mother, stepping into the hall from the kitchen, 'and you're welcome.'

*

Sam stood under the hot steamy water of the shower. His mind was everywhere. He had one hour before the first of his five meetings with the Wizard but his mind was full of this Jane woman.

Forget the woods. Forget the Wizard. Go and find her, said one voice in his head.

Sam, don't listen. Remember what the Wizard said.

The Wizard's a liar and a fraud. You know that don't you. If you go there today you'll be sucked into something behold your capacity to control. Go find Jane. You know you want to.

The confusion in his mind reminded him of an image… twisting, smothering poison ivy.

'Stop it!' he said, 'you are not going to win. I must go and find the Wizard.'

Well done, he said to himself.

It was nearly five to ten when Sam finally pulled up in the forest car park. He stepped out of the car and breathed in the country air. It was a glorious day. The sun shone down and the gentle breeze brought fresh springtide scents, floral and sweet. He made his way up the, now familiar, pathway to the Reading Chair. The Wizard was already there.

'Good morning,' said the old man, 'and what a beautiful one it is.'

'It sure is,' said Sam as the two of them shook hands.

'So have you anything you want to ask or say before we begin today's lesson?' said the Wizard.

Sam thought for a moment, bringing Jane back into his mind. He shook his head, 'No, let's just get on shall we?'

'Ok,' said the Wizard, 'why don't we sit down.'

The two men sat down side by side as the older one reached down and placed his hand inside a tatty old cloth bag near his feet. He pulled out something that looked like a small leather telescope case and set it down in the space between them.

'What is it?' asked Sam.

'Sam, inside this case is something that will look familiar yet you will have never seen one before. But before I give it to you there are some questions I need to ask you.'

'Ok, fire away,'

'Sam what is your greatest fear?'

The younger man thought for a while before answering. There seemed to be so many things that frightened him. Finally he said, 'I don't know where to begin, but I guess a life without meaning is very frightening.'

'A life without meaning! Is that where you feel you are?'

'Yes and no sir. It certainly was a few days ago. When I sat on that branch there was not one shred of meaning to my pathetic life. I felt lost and hopeless. But then I had that vision which seemed to imply I had a future and something to live for.'

The Wizard picked up the leather container and stood up. He walked a few yards away from Sam and turned round so he was facing him. 'Sam keep talking, you are close to where you need to be in order to receive this first gift.'

Sam looked up at the old man. There seemed to be an aura of light around him. 'I've always found it hard to live without a sense of purpose. I think one of the reasons why I got so deeply involved in the fellowship was that they gave purpose and meaning to my life. But it didn't last. It wasn't just my divorce that caused me to stray. In fact way before the problems between my wife and me there were questions that didn't add up.'

'Questions about the fellowship?'

'Yes. Some of their teachings began to cause me huge problems. I've rarely spoken about this. You see my mother started taking me to the fellowship meetings when I was very little and they became like a second family. I loved them, yet as I grew up I stared doubting and wondering whether some of their teachings were right. It just didn't seem to tally with what my own instincts and inner thoughts where telling me. And this gave me a constant feeling of guilt. I guess that's why I was so sympathetic to Susan when she finally left the fellowship.'

'And you felt *you* couldn't leave?'

'Leave? No the family tie was too strong. Back then there was no option, but in my heart I wanted to.'

'That must have been agony.'

Tears welled up in his eyes. The memories, the confusion, the pain all came back and it hurt.

He took out his handkerchief and wiped his eyes. 'It was awful. But Susan needed to go her own way anyway. In fact we should never really have married in the first place. We both seemed right for each other in the fellowship's eyes but I think our marriage was more to please them than ourselves. Marrying outside the fellowship was almost impossible.'

'Sam, I'm sorry this is difficult for you. But please tell me more about your need for meaning. Where do you look for meaning?'

Sam pondered the question and closed his eyes. In his mind he saw a road with a sign post. He pictured himself walking along the road with a map in his hand. 'I guess I find meaning when I know I'm on a path. When I feel I'm striving towards an answer - a goal,' he said.

'So you need to feel you are moving in order to be content? You need some sense of there being a direction and a light at the end of the tunnel?'

Yes,' said Sam opening his eyes, 'And that's how I'm feeling right now. A few days ago there was no light, no search, no direction, just a great black tunnel. In fact not even a tunnel just a hole. I'd come to the end and the end seemed a better option than just wallowing in self-pity and hopelessness'.

'Ok, Sam one more question. If you have to be moving ahead to find meaning where do you find peace?'

'Simple! I am *never* at peace,' said Sam.

The Wizard looked at the leather case in his hand and turned it so the lid was facing the sky. He unfastened a little brass clip on one side and opened it. Sam looked on with fascination.

'I want you to take this,' said the Wizard, as he stepped forward and tipped out the strange brass object. Sam took it in his right hand and studied it. It was smaller than the average telescope and did not appear to expand and contract.

'What is it?'

'For now Sam, let's leave the questions. I want you to stand up and have a good look around you, but be careful not to drop the scope.'

'Just look around?'

'Yes, just glance at anything you wish to and tell me what you see.'

Sam was confused but he did what the old man said. 'Well I can see *you* in front of me. I see the path back into the woods, and obviously trees everywhere. I think those are silver birches. I can see... oh wait what's that? I thought I saw a squirrel up there in that tree, or was it a bird?'

'Sam, now tell me please what does standing here and looking around at all this *mean* to you?'

'Mean to me? I don't know. I'm just describing ordinary things, things that I'm not really interested in. My mind is more interested in the extraordinary. I'm looking around because you told me to but I'm thinking about what I'm going to learn today.'

'Sam what if I said the answer is where you just looked?'

'I don't know what you mean,' said Sam, looking around again at what he just described.

'Ok it's time. Sam you have something in your hand. I want you to raise it to your eye, whichever one you'd normally look through. I want you to look again at the same things but through the little eye glass.'

Sam looked at the object. It was about four inches long and cylindrical.

It had a glass disk in each end and was delicately engraved with a swirling, almost paisley, pattern. He held it to his right eye and looked through.

'Oh my God!' He jumped back squinting like a fool who'd just tried to view a solar eclipse without protective eyewear.

'Don't worry,' said the old man, 'the first reaction is always shock. Go ahead look again.'

Sam rubbed his eyes with his left hand and this time very carefully raised the scope. He closed his right eye and, when the scope was in place, opened it just a fraction. The brightness and colour was intense but he gradually opened his eye until he'd become accustomed. 'Wow. I've never seen anything like it.'

'It's a kaleidoscope,' said the Wizard.

'It's not like any kaleidoscope I've seen,' replied Sam turning around and looking in wonder at the waves of colour and pulsating light oozing out of everything he looked at.

'It's one of the few original kaleidoscopes left. The ones you will have seen are completely different and rely on internal mirrors or grains of coloured glass to create the effects. They are just toys.'

'So how does this work?'

'That remains a mystery Sam. No one makes them anymore and no one, it seems, left any instructions on how they were originally made. One reason why there are so few left is that owners have been so fascinated that some have been driven to take them apart in order to discover their working, but on doing so they find they can't put them back together. But none of that's important for now Sam. Just describe the things you see.'

'I can see what look like halos around everything. Coloured halos of light that seem to throb. What does it mean?'

'Sam what you are seeing is the beauty of the here and now... the glory of the present moment. Whoever originally created these kaleidoscopes discovered a way of seeing what the vast majority of the human family normally miss. No one knows what the original intention was but it's now a priceless gift and unique symbol of something deeply profound.'

'That most of us are blind?'

'In a way, yes. Most of us have long forgotten how to live in the glory of the present moment. We fear the present because it seems so mundane. Sam your great fear is to be stuck in the apparent dull and mundane irrelevance of the here and now. That's why you always want to be moving, and can never fully rest in what is. The 'what is' is too painful for you because it feels like meaningless-ness. This kaleidoscope has been my companion for many years but I need it no more. It saved me from giving up many years ago when it was passed on in a similar fashion. It is now yours as a reminder of the colour and wonder of the now. It is symbolic though. There is much to learn about how to live in the present. It does not come easy.'

Sam stood and gazed upon the light spectrums that danced around in front of him. 'I can't believe it,' he said, 'it all looks so beautiful.'

'It all is beautiful Sam, and one day you will see that without having to use the kaleidoscope. Everything you see has an energy – a life force if you like. What the makers of this magical tool managed to do was find a way of seeing that energy. Sam, can you imagine how your life would change if you saw this energy everywhere?'

'I think I can,' he said.

'You would gradually begin to learn that the goals and achievements and answers you strive for out there are closer than you think. Indeed they are in the here and now. You would at last relax without descending into depression.'

Sam finally brought the kaleidoscope away from his eye and looked at the Wizard. For a while the colour and light was still there until it gradually faded. 'Thank you! I don't know what to say.'

'No need to thank me Sam. I just ask two things of you. Look after it, for one day you will have to pass it on, and use it every day. Each morning use the kaleidoscope for about five minutes. Look at anything you wish through it… your room, your garden, your street. It will gradually enable you to spend more time in the present and, after many years, you will find that you need to use it less. Also, as long as you're careful, carry it with you.

Whenever you find things getting too much, or depression beginning to descend, or even when you come across a difficult person, use the kaleidoscope. It will change everything like magic. Sam this is a powerful and precious tool. Guard it well and it will serve you like a true friend.'

'This is amazing,' said Sam, 'and you are quite right about me finding the mundane so difficult. I surprised myself yesterday during the drive home, when I noticed things I would normally not see.'

'There you go Sam, even without this gift you are beginning to change. That's exciting my friend.'

Sam smiled deeply. It was a smile that not only affected his mouth and face but travelled throughout his whole body. His entire physique was alive and beaming with wonder and delight.

CHAPTER 26

'So tell me Jane, are you going to go back to the psychic fayre?

It had been a long day and Jane was exhausted. All she needed now was to be hassled again by Mrs Thrip on her way home. *Oh just bugger off*. She was itching to say it out loud but her will power was strong.

'Jenny, I don't know and to be honest I really don't want to talk about it here.'

The day was long and Jane's mind was on other things. She was relieved when it came to an end and, on arriving home, decided not to call the Reader that evening. She took a shower, made herself a drink, and sat down with the cards to try and complete her unfinished notes. She read through what she'd written and added some more notes on *The Controller*.

My three cards. (left) The Controller, (centre) The Traveller, (right) True Love

First card turned - centre = the present. Subtext - The physical journey denied, a spiritual journey implied.

My notes: When plans to move are shattered a deeper force may be at work and more subtle inner movements of the soul may be taking place.

Lesson: Surrender to what is, and look for signs of growth, spiritual and emotional development.

Personal application: For whatever reason I was denied my dream of physical travel, but have been given an opportunity for a new spiritual and psychological journey. WOW.

Second card turned – left = The past / the character formed. The ego.

Subtext - Perfection's futile dream; Through cracks true light will gleam.

My notes: The hardest card to fully interpret. Much symbolism and detail. I see myself on that ladder, straining to climb and carrying the trophies of my success. Yet I also see that these trophies somehow need letting go of for their true glory to be revealed . . . the gold dust spilling out from the broken pot.

I know I am a control freak and perfectionist in every area of my life from work to relationships. The card seems to warn that such ambitious lifestyles can potentially lead to death – the dead bird frazzled by the hot sun.

The gold dust also paves the way for a journey... but it is a journey DOWN the ladder not UP higher. The truth is at the bottom. What truth is this?

Still much interpretation needed here... my thoughts continue.

Back to work today. Tough going. Heart not in it. Couldn't stop thinking of the cards all day.

I feel more and more that the card to the left is me. I am a controller. I have tried to control my life to the point where there is no room for spontaneity or fun. No room for error of failure. No room to enjoy life. In my pursuit of success I have failed at the game of life. But it's not too late. I do not need to end up a dead bird on a roof top. I need to find the gold that is at the bottom of the ladder. I'm not sure where to look but big changes are ahead. Excitement.

Still need help with this card. Will wait for Reader to advise. Now on to final card.

Jane leant back in her chair and picked up the third card, the one to the right of the spread. She read the words. *True Love*, followed by *Cling and you will kill, let go and you will keep, this is the purest love to seek.* On her day with the reader this card had proved to be most difficult of all. At least she could recognise herself in the other two. But True Love? She'd never experienced true love. All her relationships had ended in disaster.

She looked at the pictures. A man and a woman stand gazing at each other across a pond. Both with knives stuck into their backs. However both smile and stretch their arms out towards each other. They do not look frightened or sad, but content. *What is this about? Why do they look so at ease when they've been stabbed in the back?*

For a flash Jane felt a sting of rage rise within her. She knew what it was like to be stabbed in the back and when it happened all those years ago she swore never to let anyone that close again.

PART 5

'THURSDAY'

CHAPTER 27

Sam woke early. It was one of his best night's sleep in years. He'd put himself to bed at 8pm, after having dinner with his mother. She didn't quiz him or press him in any way. He'd even wondered whether she'd noticed how much better he was looking. It was now 6am and he couldn't wait for the next four hours to pass.

He sat on the side of his bed and reached over to the side cabinet. Pulling open the top draw he took out a cloth bag. Inside was another bag, a leather case. He flipped open the lid and there was his amazing gift. For a moment he held it and gazed like an enchanted child in front of a magician. Never in his life had he come across anything quite so remarkable, and it was now his own. Sam raised the scope to his eye and looked at the bedroom wall in front of him.

My God look at all the colour and vibrancy! It's amazing. He stood up and walked over to the window. Pulling back the curtains he once more placed the magic cylinder to his eye and gazed out into the street.

Look at that. Crumbs even the postman! Look at him. The postman was leaving a rainbow of coloured light behind him as he rode down the street on his bike.

CHAPTER 28

Jane had also awoken early after dreaming yet again of meeting a Wizard. She'd set her alarm even earlier because she wanted to have the time to read through her notes before going to work. The alarm had woken her just as she was leaving Oz and travelling back to Kansas with her magical red shoes.

The night before she had spent quite some time with the True Love card and had begun to understand it.

Third card turned – right = The future / unrealised potential and possibility. The True Self. True Love. Cling and you will kill, let go and you will keep, this is the purest love to seek.

At first this card angered me. My own memory of the pain. Abused trust. Broken promises. I was stabbed in the back by my first serious boyfriend. Love turned to hate. I still carry the wounds. I now see that the two souls in the picture have not wounded each other but bear the wounds of the past. Yet they have found healing by letting go of hatred and letting go of the need for possessive love.

Jane stopped reading for a moment.

Gosh where did I get all that from? She was surprised by her analysis and reading of the card. Then she remembered something the Reader said to her at the Psychic Fayre:

'My child. Every once in a while I meet someone who *knows*. I don't wish to frighten you but I feel that you will be able to read the cards for yourself.'

She read on.

...letting go of the need for possessive love. The two lovers can love because they are free and the space between them symbolises their ability to love without clinging... to possess love without being possessed by love.

Will I ever find this kind of love? God knows I long for it but all the men I've met since him have never coped with my coldness... the fact that I can't let them close in case they hurt me. Again I see myself as a controller.

Also a goal of a human life is to love Self.

Other features of the card: ripples in the pond, something golden and glowing in the centre of the pond beneath the water, the space between the two characters is a different colour to the rest of the card – a hazy blue colour. Not sure yet what any of these features represent.

Jane sat there for a while looking over her notes and wondering where it was all leading. Then she remembered her dream.

Dorothy again! Well I guess I do feel a little like her. But where's the Wizard? Oh of course the Reader! Perhaps she's my Wizard of Oz. Yet another part of Jane thought the Reader was more like the good witch of the North who occasionally appeared in a bubble to guide young Dorothy. And the three cards were of course the three fellow travellers.

So maybe there is a Wizard still to come? In fact she knew exactly why she was having this dream and it was all very rational. She'd always loved the film as a child and had simply been reminded of it, that's all. It just happened to symbolise, quite beautifully, some of the experiences she was having, but it was nothing more than that. Or was it?

CHAPTER 29

'Hello again Sam,' said the Wizard as the younger man approached, 'you look happier today, if I may say so.'

'And I feel so,' said Sam.

The Wizard stood and greeted Sam with a hand shake and a pat on his shoulder. 'Today Sam, we go deeper, but it might be a little painful.'

Sam looked at him with eagerness, 'Whatever, I'm ready. I've never been so certain of anything in my life.'

'A reasonable amount of caution is always wise Sam. Don't let your euphoria run away with you. In life things can turn at any point, especially when you are on a spiritual journey. The ego can't stand you growing like this. It will fight you, so be warned and prepare yourself.'

He turned in the opposite direction from the path that Sam had just followed and beckoned him to follow.

'Where are we going then?' said Sam.

'We're going deeper into your inner world, and to help us do that we'll go deeper into the forest.'

'But there's no pathway?'

'Exactly' said the Wizard.

The two men walked to the edge of the clearing around the Reading Chair. There was the tiniest opening but it looked far too small for a fully grown man to squeeze through. The old man looked at Sam who showed signs of concern.

'Are we going in *there?*' said Sam, pointing at the crack in the dense bush.

'Yes,' said the Wizard, 'follow me.' With that the old man leant forward and, arms held out in front of him, squeezed into the gap. It took a bit of effort but he soon pushed through. Sam followed.

'Ouch,' said the younger man as something sharp and spiky stuck in his side.

'Keep going,' said the old man,' It won't take long.'

'I hope you know what you're doing,'

'Trust me.'

The two men continued pushing and squeezing their way into the dense wood of the forest. There was the sound of small animals scurrying away and the snapping of ground twigs. It was dark. After a few minutes the Wizard paused.

'What is it?' said Sam.

'Listen,' said the old man, 'can you here that?' Sam strained to hear what the Wizard was speaking of but it just seemed totally silent.

'I can't hear a thing', he whispered.

'Exactly! Isn't it marvellous? No sounds, nothing to distract us from the moment.' The Wizard stood perfectly still for a few more seconds then looked round at Sam, 'Come on then, we're nearly there.'

Suddenly, after one more uncomfortable push, they were back out into the light again. It was another forest clearing. There was a canopy above but it was not so dense and light filtered through the branches and leaves.

Sam looked around, 'Wow, how did you know this was here?'

'Oh I've been here before,' said the Wizard.

They walked into the centre of the clearing. It reminded Sam of a crop circle. It was perfectly round, but what Sam couldn't work out was that it seemed to have grown that way. There was no sign of human design. No evidence of tree stumps or bruised ground.

The Wizard removed his long coat and spread it out on the ground. 'Lie down!' he said.

'Lie down?' What... here?'

'Yes... please just lie down and look up into the leaves above.'

Sam knew there was no point asking too many questions. He'd already learned that the Wizard would only answer what he wanted to. He'd also picked up that he enjoyed leaving Sam with a sense of mystery and unanswered-ness. *Clever man knows just what an analyser I am. Even now he's trying to re-train me.* Sam's admiration for the man grew rapidly. He'd never come across such a person before.

'Ok,' said Sam, lying down and gazing up into the green canopy above, 'what now?'

'Just lie there for a while… don't think…don't ask… don't *try* to understand. Just lie there and take it in.'

Telling Sam not to think and question was like telling a puppy not to wag its tail and pant but he did his best. Then it started to happen…

What's that? Sam felt something under his head and twitched instinctively. *Must be a bug or a worm under the coat.* Just then a loud crashing noise came from the left. *Who's there?* Then the same noise came from the other side. Sam sat up and turned to the Wizard who was sat a few feet away behind where his head had lain.

'Did you hear that?'

'Sam, trust me and lie back down. Don't think or question. Just take in the experiences. I need you to do this before we begin the real lesson for today.'

Once more Sam lay down and before long it started again. The earth creaked under his head. There were noises like falling trees to his left and right. Tremors and quakes rippled under every part of his body. Then he saw movement in the trees above him, strange movements, shapes and forms darting around, patterns and waves of colour and light.

The Wizard spoke, 'Sam this is a continuation of yesterday's lesson. Stay where you are for a while and describe what you are experiencing.'

'It's like the whole world's alive. I can hear noises all round me and there's movement under my head and body. Up there above is movement too… things too far away to see normally. What's happening?'

'Did you use your kaleidoscope this morning?'

'Yes, for five minutes, like you told me to.'

'Good, it's beginning to happen then.'

'What is?'

'Sam you spend most of your life in the future. Yet the future does not exist... neither does the past, which is another place you visit regularly. The only place that exists is the present. As you know the gift you received yesterday will show you the true nature of the present whenever you use it, and over time it will correct the bad habits you've formed. But today, here, right now, even without that eyeglass, you are experiencing more of that glorious present than you ever have before.'

'So is this real?'

'Yes Sam it's real. What you are sensing is precisely what you just described –the whole world is indeed alive.'

'Is the earth under me breathing then?'

'In a way, yes. Sam what you can hear and feel and see is all the life that lives on Mother Earth. Lying still and stopping has simply made you more aware of the ceaseless activity that most humans are never conscious of. You've been listening to the world of the invisible creatures. You've heard the burrowing and the creating of passageways. You felt the shifting of the earth as the worms and centipedes pushed their way through. Under them are the bigger burrowing animals and these too, you could feel. The sounds to your left and right are like the falling of trees but in reality it was simply the bending and breaking of tiny twigs and blades of grass as a vole no bigger than your little finger darted past you.'

'And above me. What are the movements I can see?'

'Above you, Sam, is the life of the canopy. You are seeing the countless millions of creatures... all active in their daily tasks. Each one of them, the semi-visual and the microscopic, have their place in the design of the planet.'

'It's amazing,' said Sam, 'and quite beautiful.'

'It is indeed. If only people took more time for this kind of meditation they'd live much fuller and more positive lives.'

'I could stay like this forever,' said Sam.

'I know,' said the Wizard, 'however I have something I need to give you now so, when you feel ready, would you like to sit up. And, remember, you can do what you just did any time you wish.'

Sam rolled on to his side and pushed himself up so he could kneel. He then stood to his feet and stretched. When he looked at the Wizard he noticed he was holding something. It looked like an old fashioned metal cine film container. Sam remembered the last time he saw such an object.

*

He was about ten years old and he and his best friend Bobby had been rummaging around in the attic of Sam's house. Bobby was one of the handful of Sam's friends who were not part of the fellowship. Bobby lived next door to Sam and, though they attended different schools, the boys got to know each other after Bobby's parents had invited Sam and his mother for a Christmas drink a few years earlier. The adults clashed badly, partly because of Sam's mother's hostile comments with regard to alcohol, but Sam and Bobby clicked and a friendship was born. One of the most distressing events Sam had to deal with as a teenager was the tragic news of Bobby's death after a horrific accident involving a motorcycle. Of all things the bike was his parents' 17th birthday gift. No one knew how it happened but poor Bobby's mangled body was found in a field about five miles out of town, his head twisted 180 degrees.

However the memory that Sam had in his mind was of the day they found Sam's late father's old film projector. Before long the two boys had set it up and it worked. They were in the middle of watching a film of Sam as a baby when his mother burst into the room shouting at the top of her voice.

'What are you doing?' she screamed, 'You should know better than to go digging around into things that don't belong to you.'

But, mother.'

'Don't you "but mother" me. These films are private... they should never be watched.'

'Mother they're of me.'

'No they're not, they're of... oh... look just get out both of you.'

Sam and Bobby ran out of the room while she put everything back into the box to hide away in a place it would never be found.

Sam's mother was plagued with a quick temper but he'd always wondered why she was so enraged about that cine film.

It wasn't until many years later that Sam eventually discovered why his mother had acted that way. His parents had had another son before Sam, but he died as an infant. It was his brother in the cine film not Sam. He always suspected whether he had been his parents' attempt to fill the void left after his brother's death...

*

'Sam,' said the Wizard.

The younger man blinked and looked up, 'Sorry, I was somewhere else. That thing you're holding. It reminded me of something.'

'This is your second gift Sam. I'm going to give it to you but I do not want you to open it or do anything with it for a while. Ok.'

Sam held out his hand and took the metal container, 'Thanks.'

'Don't thank me just yet Sam. This might be difficult for you. Let's sit down on my coat... but hold on to that without moving it at all if you can.'

What the hell's he given me? Sam looked down and studied the object in his hands, which were now trembling. *Steady Sam. Come on stay calm.* With great care and watching each inch of ground like a hawk he paced the few feet needed to reach the long coat and knelt down. Still holding onto the object he repositioned one leg, and then the other until he was sat crossed legged holding the tin in his lap.

'What the hell is this thing?'

'Hell indeed,' said the Wizard with a gentle smile, 'It may just be *hell*, but that depends on you.'

'What do you mean?'

'Sam, what do *you* think that tin contains?'

'How should I know? Whatever it is it's beginning to frighten me.'

'Why? Why does it frighten you?'

'Because you are making me nervous,' he said, 'you've suggested that it's dangerous.'

'No Sam. You've allowed yourself to imagine it's dangerous.'

'Forgive me for correcting you but did you not just say that it might be hell for me, and before that didn't you tell me not to thank you just yet, and that I was to hold it very carefully without moving it all it. You've made it sound like I'm holding nitro-glycerine.'

'Sam, this is the beginning of today's lesson. Try to stay with me. Try to understand. Now you have just taken some of my words and used them to create imaginary fears. What I actually said to you when you thanked me for the gift was this: "Don't thank me just yet Sam. This might be difficult for you. Let's sit down on my coat... but hold on to that without moving it at all if you can."'

'I *know* that's what you said. Isn't that telling me the box is dangerous?'

'No Sam. What I was saying is that what this gift is going to teach you may well be unsettling, so don't be too quick to thank me for it. The reason for me asking you to hold it still will become apparent in a moment. But it's not because the box itself is dangerous.'

'And what did you mean by hell?'

'I repeated your use of the word hell Sam because what so often goes on in your mind is precisely that – hell. Look, I just ask you to trust me. It *will* become clear.'

'Ok,' said Sam still trembling,' What do you want me to do.'

'Hold up the tin and begin to shake it, ever so slightly.'

Sam looked as though he'd been asked to place his hand in a tank of piranhas. *What shake a tin of nitro-glycerine? Is he mad?* His face gave him away.

'Sam, it's alright. Please just shake the tin. Sam, think about it. How could I have brought it here if it were literally explosive?'

Sam held the container in his right hand and looked hard at it. It was about the size of a tin of boot polish and looked like solid silver. He also noticed an engraving on the lid but it was hard to make out what it depicted.

He quickly realised the image was upside down and carefully turned it the right way. *What the hell?* Again, he'd used the right word. His inner voice had expressed exactly what the image depicted. It was an engraving of some sort of monster with scales, horns, huge sharp teeth and flames exuding from its mouth.

'What's this?' he said looking at the image as if the monster was real.

'It's an image to induce fear.'

'It's good at its job,' said Sam, 'but why? Why to induce fear?'

'Sam this is called a phobia box. Like the kaleidoscope there aren't many left today. Even though it looks quite new it's about three hundred years old. It's just been looked after with great care. These things were originally made as rich man's toys, but people began to realise their psychological potential, even though it wouldn't have been called that in those days. The inventor sold his rights to a particular aristocratic German family, who eventually produced them in the form of this one. Sam you are holding a remarkable object. Now, please give it a little shake.'

Sam was still transfixed by the image. It looked like all his worst nightmares rolled into one... the detail was magnificent and the malevolence intense. He very carefully rocked it. *Clang!*

'Oh my God! What was that?' It sounded as thought it was coming from somewhere else, a deep echoic sound, but Sam knew the noise came from within the box. He rocked it again but this time with a bit more force. *Clang. Thud.* The sounds were accompanied by the sensation of a heavy solid objects crashing around inside the box. Yet it occurred to Sam that the box was rather light. Sam was intrigued. *How can this be? What's inside? Why does it feel and sound so huge and so heavy?*

'Now Sam, go ahead and shake it.'

Sam shook the box. The noise was louder still and menacing. It felt alive, like a metallic beetle scurrying around.

'What is this thing?' cried Sam, 'It really scares me'.

'It's supposed to,' said the Wizard, 'now, are you ready to open it?'

CHAPTER 30

At last the clock's two hands joined at the highest point and the gongs that signalled 12 noon struck. Jane was now free for an hour.

Thank God.

After signing out she hurried from the store and dived into her car that was parked in the company car park.

Ok. Let's see where we are with all this.

On her left hand passenger seat were the sandwiches and flask of coffee she'd prepared early and in the glove compartment were the three cards and note book. She put her hand down to the right side of the driver's seat and pulled a leaver. She then Pushed with her legs and the chair moved backwards giving her a little more space.

'Hello my friends,' she said, as she placed the three cards face up on the dash board in front of her.

CHAPTER 31

Sam held the phobia box dragon side up. Sweat ran down his forehead into his eyes. The Wizard looked on, waiting for him to open the box.

'Come on Sam, this is a test. I know you can do it.'

'Oh God,' he said with his eyes closed and head turned away as if he were holding a hand grenade with the pin pulled out.

'Sam, why can't you open it?'

'I'm petrified,' he said, 'I feel like I'm holding an encased demon or something. Whatever's in here will be terrifying... I'm certain of it.'

'How are you certain?'

'The image. The thoughts in my head. The sounds. The feelings for God's sake. It's not natural... this box. Look I can't do it.' All of Sam's fears plagued his mind. Devilish monsters rushed through his head causing havoc. Then the voices started... first the critical then the calm. The mental argument was unleashed.

Sam. Don't open the box. It's full of poison; spiritual poison that will pollute you for ever. You'll be lost – thrown into hell if you open it.

Calm down. Remember how far you've come. The Wizard has every-thing under control. This is all part of the lesson. Trust and all will be well.

Sam, come on, you know what you should do. This man's evil. Get away from him while it's still possible. If you open that box you'll be face to face with the devil from hell.

No, stop it. Don't get confused. Don't listen.

Sam suddenly remembered the Wizard's words about his voices. He was scared. He didn't want to do it. But he also knew that the right option was to do as the Wizard said. He looked once more at the horrific image on the lid and clasped the tin with both hands.

'Sam, before you prize it open I have to ask you, what do you think is inside?'

Sam gulped before answering, 'I don't know. But it's frightening the hell out of me. I can't remember being so scared of something I can't see before.'

'Are you sure about that Sam?'

'Yes. I think so anyway.'

He shut his eyes tight and held the tin between his two hands. As the tin turned on its side there was one almighty crash coming from within…. A huge bead of sweat ran down the side of Sam's face and onto his neck near the wound. Briefly there was a flash of pain caused by the salt entering the recent cut. One huge pull and *Pap!* The container opened.

CHAPTER 32

Jane nibbled the corner of a salmon and cucumber sandwich. *Ok, True Love, where did I get with you?*

*

By the end of her lunch break she'd added a few more pages to her notes on the third card, and something had surprised her even as she wrote it. Before going back in for the afternoon shift she re-read the notes so far:

Third card turned – right = The future / unrealised potential and possibility. The True Self. True Love. Cling and you will kill, let go and you will keep, this is the purest love to seek.

At first this card angered me. My own memory of the pain. Abused trust. Broken promises. I was stabbed in the back by my first serious boyfriend. Love turned to hate. I sill carry the wounds. I now see that the two souls in the picture have not wounded each other but bear the wounds of the past. Yet they have found healing by letting go of hatred and letting go of the need for possessive love. The two lovers can love because they are free and the space between them symbolises their ability to love without clinging... to possess love without being possessed by love.

Will I ever find this kind of love? God knows I long for it but all the men I've met since him have never coped with my coldness... the fact that I can't let them close in case they hurt me. Yet again I see myself as a controller.

Also a goal of a human life is to love Self.

Other features of the card: ripples in the pond, something golden and glowing in the centre of the pond beneath the water, the space between the two characters is a different colour to the rest of the card –

a hazy blue colour. Not sure yet what any of these features represent.

Notes on Thursday – lunch break:

Today I am drawn to the gold glittering beneath the surface of the pond. What can it mean? My instincts tell me it speaks of a treasure yet to be discovered. It is a hidden treasure that exists within the space between two lovers. Gold seems to be everywhere. I am dreaming of following a yellow golden pathway to meet a Wizard. Gold is spilled down the ladder in the Controller card. Gold exists at the bottom of the ladder too... Oh my God. I've just seen it. I am to be given another chance. There will be another relationship for me, but the gold will not be locked away inside him but between us, within our spaces as well as our being together. I put all my eggs in one basket before and when it fell apart protected myself by building a great wall and setting out to climb a huge ladder of perfection and success. The overseas job would have been the pathway to every success I dreamed of, yet inside I would have remained lonely for I was climbing away from myself. The cards were right. The traveller card spoke of a new beginning... a spiritual journey. I can now safely say I've accepted the journey even though I still don't know where it leads.

The controller card showed me who I was becoming but also that my salvation is not up there at the top, where the sun shines brightly (where the dead bird lies) but down at the bottom, where the cracked pot lies spilling out gold.

It's all tying together now. My God it seems Jenny Thrip had an important place in my life after all. I still wonder about this Wizard? Perhaps it's simply a dream, after all I'd reminded myself of my favourite childhood movie. It was bound to show up in my dreams.

As Jane closed her journal she reminded herself of a conversation she'd had with the Reader on their first meeting:

"'I can't see what you are seeing, but I can help you to uncover what

your inner voice is trying to tell you.'

'What are you, a clairvoyant or a shrink?'

'Neither, my role is that of a Reader. I know these cards and the messages they whisper. They speak because they resonate deeply with the human soul. They have no power of their own but connect with your inner self. They can be like signposts on an inner journey.'"

Jane *remember that*, she cautioned herself, *these cards do not see into the future. They enable you to see your life as it is... like little symbolic mirrors. You must not start to believe they are telling your fortune.* With that final thought she knew she had to contact the Reader again, and made plans to see her that evening.

CHAPTER 33

Nothing? Sam peered into the tin, and then into its upturned lid. He looked at the Wizard, who was smiling.

'Sam you look confused.'

'Confused! For God's sake what do you expect? Where is it? Where's the thing that made all the noise and thudded around so much?'

The Wizard turned away and walked towards the edge of the clearing.

What the hell is he doing now? Sam followed after him. They both stood with their backs to the thick of the wood facing inwards to the centre of the circle.

'Look' said the Wizard, pointing at something.

'Please, I can't concentrate until I know where that object went.'

'I'm going to show you,' said the Wizard, 'look, that's where you lay down not so long ago.' He pointed to the coat lying on the floor in the centre of the circle.

'So?'

'When you lay on the floor you heard and felt things that were huge didn't you?'

'Yes.'

'Yet when you sat up you realised they were tiny, and usually invisible to most people.'

'Yes, ok, but what's that got to do with the object in the box?'

'Right now what is there in this space here in this clearing?'

'What, apart from you and I? Nothing much!'

'Right and wrong Sam.'

'Explain!'

'Right now within this space are more things you cannot see. Just like those tiny creatures that made all that sound, every square centimetre of this space is filled with life and with energy. Just because you can't see it does not mean it isn't there.'

'Ok. Sure, I get that, but what on earth has that got to do with the object on the box?'

'Sam there is no object.'

'What it's just vanished into thin air?'

'No there is no object and there was no object.'

'Bloody hell. Now I'm *really* confused.'

'Sam if it's possible to believe that this clearing, thought seemingly empty, is in reality full of life and energy, can't it also be possible that a small tin box that seems full is in reality empty?'

'They are two totally different things. We are talking about a scientific fact about this space here and the microscopic life that lives invisibly within it. But that container? Well it's just impossible. I felt it and heard it. Something *was* inside.'

'Sam I gave it to you because it's a profound symbol, and it too has a scientific answer. It's just that no one living knows what it is. It's a very clever invention Sam, an Eighteenth Century precision made magic trick. I told you it was bought and modified by a family of German psychologists. They called it a phobia box because of the effect it had on people… people just like you. They manufactured a hand full of them for others who worked with the human mind, especially with people who suffered from uncontrollable fears and phobias. They made them with the horrific engraving to achieve a quicker association with what their clients thought was on the inside. Great tales of miracle healings were shared. Stories were told of people who'd been trapped inside their frightened minds for years being delivered as if by magic. Apparently they'd be given a box and asked to look at the image on it. Then they'd be instructed to close their eyes and imagine their greatest fear… to actually see it… personify it. After a few moments of this they'd be directed to gently shake the tin and feel the object roll and bang around inside. Hypnotherapy, as such, was not practised officially but the therapists would actively encourage their clients to see their object of fear as now existing within the box and, as it jagged and crashed around, to see it grow. As they did this they would shake it harder and harder and it would feel bigger and the noise would become intense. Then, at the point of most terror, the quasi-hypnotist would force open the tin – still being held in the client's hands – where upon they would discover that is was totally empty. Sometimes the fears and phobias that had haunted people for years disappeared immediately on opening the box… as if it was saying, "your fear seems so real… so solid… so true … yet it is based upon nothing." Sam, would you put the lid back on the box.'

Sam looked in awe at the tin box, 'ok,' he said.

'Now gently rock it again.'

As he did so the sound echoed around the clearing.

'How on earth does this work?'

'Sam, don't ask questions just follow my instructions. I want you to see that even though you now know the secret, this little box can *still* be your friend and helper. I want you to begin shaking the box in your right hand and, this time, allow your mind to drift. Ask your imagination to carry you to a place of fear and raise your left hand when you have done that.'

Sam did as he was told and eventually raised his left hand. Ok you have found a fear. Now see it. Make it concrete. If it is a real person then make him or her into a statue and mentally place them in the box. If it's a phobia, like heights or spiders then try to picture it – a cliff top or a tarantula. Put whatever you are thinking into that box. Good. The fear is in the box. It seems real. It has control of areas of your life. It is heavy – it feels heavy. It is loud and echoes round this clearing. It's in your hands Sam. You have your fear in your own hand. That must be scary. Are you scared?'

'Bloody hell yes.'

'Sam open your eyes and, if you dare, try and face your fear… open the box NOW.'

Sam knew it was empty but the meditation had made it seem so real. And there really was something there – he could feel it… but he did as the Wizard commanded and opened the box. *Nothing.*

'Nothing. There's nothing here – yet it feels so real, even more real this time.'

'Sam this is your second gift. You are a fearful man. You fear night and day yet most of your fears are based on thin air. Your fears are in your mind Sam. This phobia box will be a constant reminder of that until you need it no more. It will take time – years in fact. So don't think you'll get there in a week. And you can do that exercise we just did whenever you discover a new fear… for there are countless phobias and fears that plague your soul.'

'Thank you,' said Sam, looking shattered and phased.

'Let's go back now and we'll get some lunch together. Then we'll call it a day and meet again tomorrow.'

CHAPTER 34

'Ok, see you tomorrow evening then, thank you.'

'I look forward to it my dear,' said the Reader.

Jane was looking forward to a hot bath and an early night. She put the phone down and walked into the bathroom. The room was full of sweetly scented steam and the bath was nearly full. She bent over, tested the water, and turned the hot tap off. After allowing a few more trickles of cold she was ready. *Ahhh Luxury.*

PART 6

'FRIDAY'

CHAPTER 35

Sam woke at around 8am. The night before he'd enjoyed another pleasant meal with his mother but he couldn't work her out. Was she calming down because she saw a change for the better in him, or was she just trying to tolerate his journeys to the wood until he got over it and returned to the fellowship? He didn't know which. And, right now, he didn't care.

Sam yawned, stretched and swung his feet round so he could sit up on the edge of the bed. He looked at his bedside cabinet and slid open the top draw. *My two priceless gifts!*

'Sam! Sam… would you like a cooked breakfast?'

Cooked breakfast? She hasn't made me one of those in years. 'Um, yes please mother. That would be great. Thank you'.

*

Sam had been living back with his mother since the divorce. He always felt he was something of a burden to her not just practically but emotionally too. He could sense her embarrassment when people called round from the fellowship and saw him there. He often wondered why she didn't just throw him out or why she even took him back in the first place. She obviously disapproved of the divorce and agreed with the verdict of the elders.

So what's happening now, he thought as she busied herself with his bacon, eggs and fried tomatoes?

*

Two hours later he was back with the Wizard.

'Hello,' said Sam as he approached the familiar figure sat on the Reading Chair.

'Good morning,' said the Wizard, 'how did you sleep?'

'Very well,' said Sam, 'In fact, thinking about it, very well indeed.'

*

One of the most frustrating and, at times, soul destroying area's of Sam's life was his sleep pattern. He never understood why he had such a problem with sleep. It was not that he didn't want to... he just couldn't. He occasionally used to try to think back to a time or occasion when he slept like a baby, but he couldn't remember any. His mother once told him that even as a baby he never slept like one. She'd be up eight or ten times a night, and it wasn't for feeding or nappy changing. He was just a restless infant. And it never got any better. His sleep deprivation became most intense during the years leading up to his divorce, which added to the depression and constant feeling of physical and mental fatigue. Since then there had been various periods where the gaps between sleep were fewer and shorter, but this was largely due to the huge 'night caps' he'd began relying on.

*

'Gosh,' said Sam, as he quickly calculated something in his head, 'It's just occurred to me that I haven't taken a drink for five nights now?'

'You drink?'

Sam sat down beside the Wizard. 'Doesn't everyone?'

'What do you drink Sam?'

'Oh it's not a problem, at least not yet. I usually need half a tumbler of scotch before bed. I have trouble sleeping and a shot of the hard stuff will give me a few hours.'

'But you haven't done that for five nights?'

'No, no I haven't'

'Why do think that is Sam?'

He thought for a while and allowed his mind to drift back over the past few days. 'Well on the first night, the Sunday, I was exhausted and had to be put to bed by my mother. I think I was asleep even before I hit the sheets. The next night was after I'd met you. I was so confused but I had achieved something I'd never managed in my life...

'Which was?'

'I stood up to the Minister... and to the whole damn fellowship.'

'And how did that make you feel?'

'Well, elated and strong. Because of the confusion and the voices in my head I was still very unsure about you, but I'd make a decision and stood my ground. I have never been so assertive to someone who fills me with such fear. And I felt good... even peaceful. I think that's why I slept without the need of a drink.'

'How well did you sleep that night?'

Sam thought for a moment, 'Not like a log but better than I'm used to and, without taking whisky, I'd say that was pretty good.'

'And the rest of the week?'

'Like I said, I haven't needed a drink and each night's been deeper sleep. But last night was incredible. It was the best night's sleep I've ever had. I feel great.'

'That's good Sam. You are doing so well. Yesterday's lesson was quite traumatic but it removed some of your inner fear and paranoia. That's why you slept so well. More will come in that area, but today I'm going to set you a test, and if you pass the test you will find something that will bring with it the highest level of peace.'

'I can't wait,' said Sam, 'what's the test?'

The Wizard stood and looked at Sam. 'Sam, today I'm sending you on a treasure hunt.'

CHAPTER 36

Jane stood in her cosmetic department watching the shoppers pass, but her mind was somewhere else completely. Suddenly she saw someone she recognised.

'Hello Jane,' said the tall man as he strode up to her.

'Dan,' she didn't know whether to smile or scowl, 'my God, how are you? And what are you doing here?'

'Oh I was just passing the store and glanced in. I thought it was you. Hope you don't mind… it's been ages.'

'*Years* Dan. What are you doing with yourself these days?'

'Tell you the truth Jane, not a lot.'

You never did, thought Jane, 'Not got a job then? What about family? Did you ever…?'

'Marry? No, you know me.'

Yes I know you. I bloody know you too well don't I. 'Still travelling the world and living off your parents' money then are we?'

'Ouch!'

'I'm sorry Dan. It's just a real shock to see you and…'

'I know. You don't have to apologise. It's me who needs to apologise. Look, how about I treat you to dinner tonight?'

Jane looked incredulous. *Is he for real?*

'I can't,' she said, 'I'm seeing someone.'

Dan's face changed, the cheesy smile replaced by a look of disappointment, 'seeing someone? Oh'

'Not like that Dan. It's just a… oh you'd never understand. Look I haven't "seen anyone" since you and I finished.'

'Another night then?'

'Sure. It would be good to catch up but Dan I'm really not…'

He didn't let her finish, 'Great, here's my number. Call me when you can. I don't live too far away now. Just moved back to my folks' place.'

I bet you have. And I bet they're REAL happy about that. 'Ok Dan, will do.'

The handsome man smiled and turned to leave. Then, before walking away, whispered with just enough volume, 'You're still as sexy as ever.' And he was gone.

So are you, thought Jane.

CHAPTER 37

Sam had received his instructions and was on his way holding a hand drawn map. Over his shoulder hung a bag containing a hard boiled egg, some cheese sandwiches and a bottle of water provided by the Wizard.

'For the journey,' he'd said, 'It won't be easy and it could take a huge chunk of the day'.

His task was to find the point marked on the map with a cross and uncover a hidden box, inside of which would be his third gift. However he had been given no spade or tool of any sort. 'All will be made clear' the Wizard had told him, 'as long as you remain open.'

Gosh he really wants me to work for this one.

The map reminded him of a game he used to play with Bobby. One of them would make a treasure map and the other would have to uncover clues and find the treasure, which might be a biscuit or piece of chocolate.

He chuckled to himself. *Gosh if Bobby could see me now!* As he walked on so he reminisced about how good life was with his little friend.

*

One of the things Sam liked most about Bobby was that he seemed so free. He had not had the misfortune of growing up inside the claustrophobia of a heavily religious family. In a way Sam envied Bobby for this. On one occasion, when they were about fifteen years old, Bobby asked Sam a question he would never forget. They'd ridden out into the country and were leaning over a bridge throwing sticks into a stream when Bobby spoke.

'Sam,' he said, 'why do you believe all that crap?'

'What,' Sam looked around to see if anyone could hear, then whispered very sharply, 'what *crap* Bobby?'

'Well all that stuff from your church. I know other people who belong to churches but they don't believe all the stuff you lot do.'

'Well *they* are not true believers then *are they?*'

'You see, *that's* the crap I'm talking about. You lot really think you're the only ones who've got it right don't you.'

'Bobby. Where's all this coming from?'

This was the very first time the two friends had ever discussed Sam's religious side. They'd always managed to avoid it, partly because Sam loved the freedom of having at least one friend who was not part of the fellowship. He enjoyed not having to talk about it. And Bobby was just uninterested. But on this occasion something had prompted him to ask a question and it had put them both on edge.

'I'm sorry Sam. It's just that my parents were talking about it and they said your mum won't have anything to do with them because they are going to hell. Is that what they really think Sam? Is that what you think? Do you believe I am going to hell?'

Sam turned and looked at his best friend. He wished he hadn't asked him this. Bobby turned and the two boys stood eye-to-eye, each one with a face more serious than the other had seen before. Finally Sam spoke.

'I really don't know what I think Bobby. It's what *they* say. They say all sorts of things about people who don't belong to the fellowship. They don't even think I should be friends with you. I find it so hard because I *do* believe. I've grown up with it you see. I feel like there's someone out there protecting me.'

'But Sam do you believe like your mother does... that my family are going to hell?'

Sam looked deeply into Bobby's eyes. Both their faces displayed sadness. Sam didn't have to say a word. They both knew what he thought. From that day on there was a barrier between the two boys. Something had broken between them. It would never be the same again.

*

'Bugger those bastards,' Sam shouted out as he walked on. His memories had changed his mood. He was angry. 'They robbed me of my best friend. Why did I allow them to twist my mind like that?'

He stopped walking and looked up into the branches above. 'God, I do believe in you, but why do your people make it so hard? Why did I have to grow up in the fellowship? Why couldn't I have belonged to a different church? I *know* they're not all like ours. God I miss him. I miss Bobby so much and I'll never see him again. Why?'

The troubled man wiped the tears from his eyes and looked down at the map in his hand. *Bobby's with you now Sam,* said a voice in his head. *Bobby will always be with you in spirit.*

No he won't he's in hell.

No Sam. He's with God. Sam remembered the Wizard's words about which voice to trust. 'Yes, God, he *is* with you. I *know* he is.'

He continued to follow the route. It was a simple path with no obstacles.

What kind of a treasure hunt is this? Even a three year old boy could pass this test, he thought as he walked on.

CHAPTER 38

'Thank you! Have a nice day,' said Jane, as she watched the woman walk away with a carrier bag. Then her mind returned to where it was a few moments before.

Imagine that! 'Dan Shaw back! She cautioned herself. *Jane be careful, you know what he's like.*

It was almost mid-day and Jane told herself to put Dan's image to one side for a while. She'd got more important things to do.

*

Ten minutes later Jane was sat back in her car. The lunch box was to her left and the three cards were standing neatly on the dash board. She had her note book in hand.

Now what do I need to check with the Reader tonight?

She turned to a clean page and wrote some questions that had occurred to her since her last glance at the cards.

Things to ask the Reader:

Are the cards ever able to forecast events? And if not why does it seem like they are doing that for me?

And what about Dan? I'm scared. This man has power over me... emotional and sexual power. What do I do? I don't want to be sucked in to his world again... yet (if I'm honest) part of me does.

CHAPTER 39

Sam had walked for roughly two hours and, even with a full English breakfast inside him, he was beginning to get hungry. *Time to stop for a bite.*

He sat down on the trunk of a fallen tree and opened his lunch bag. The food was just what he needed after two hours walking. He was surprised by the size of the wood and looked again at the map. As far as he could work out he was just supposed to follow one single pathway marked as a dotted line on the map. It was basically a straight line though it had a few dips and bends. The man-made gravel path of the manufactured wood had long since disappeared, but there was a clear natural footpath to follow. The map showed the destination as being a large object of some description, where the X was drawn on the map. The object itself was unclear but its location could be identified by three huge fir trees to one side and an even bigger one to the other. They had been drawn on the map in a flat medieval style to show their height. They reminded Sam of something he'd seen before but couldn't think where.

I wonder how much further it's going to be? thought Sam as he swallowed a large mouthfull of water. One thing that was unclear about the map was the scale. It had been drawn like a child's map so the reference points and markers were all out of proportion. The line he'd been instructed to follow could be five miles or twenty.

Hope it's not too far now! Gotta find the damn thing and then walk all the way back!

Sam finished his lunch and decided to get going. He glanced at his watch. It was 12.30. Suddenly a thought occurred to him.

Oh God I haven't passed the place have I?

At no point had he noticed four huge fir trees, but the forest was dense so he probably wouldn't have. However he comforted himself with the thought that he hadn't passed any unusual object either and, had he done so, he would have definitely noticed.

More minutes passed, then hours until it was 2pm.

'Come on, it must be close now', he said out loud as he glanced at his watch.

You fool Sam. Can't you see what's happening. He's leading you on a wild goose chase. You'd better turn back.

No I won't listen to you. I'm going to find this gift. I know it's here somewhere.

Sam was getting tired and he was finding it hard to quieten the negative voice in this head.

You'll see. You'll be here for days before you find any hidden treasure.

The path had dipped and risen a few times along the walk but now Sam faced a hill. It was still wooded but he could see the path begin to rise. He looked up, exhausted. *How much longer?*

He frowned at the map again. *No bloody hills there? Surely a real hill would have been marked.? It would be an obvious marker for shit's sake. Oh God I really have gone wrong haven't I?*

I told you that ages ago but you wouldn't listen you stubborn fool.

Sam stopped. He had no idea what to do. He was so tired now and couldn't bear the thought of walking on up that hill, especially if he was going to have to walk all the way back.

What do I do?

Turn back!

Or should I just walk this final stretch and then decide when I get to the top?

No. Turn back you damn fool. The negative voice shouted and stomped inside his head like a spoilt child.

Sam remember which voice the Wizard said to trust.

'Ok', he said audibly, 'I'll go on, but if there's still nothing after this hill I turn back.'

Sam paced on. The hill was steep, each step adding to the fatigue in his legs and back.

Only a bit further.

The footpath led him up until at last the ground flattened out and he knew he'd reached the top. He lifted his head and, though the wood obscured a totally clear view, he could see down the other side of the hill. There before him, only about five minutes walk away, stood three huge fir trees in a group and, to their right, an even higher one.

CHAPTER 40

Jane looked at her watch. *Oh come on.* She willed the hands to move faster. It was only mid-afternoon and she wasn't going to see the Reader until the evening. The day couldn't pass quick enough for her.

CHAPTER 41

Not far now, thought Sam.

Since seeing the four great fir trees he felt a new burst of energy. He marched on towards his destination. As he descended, the woods became thicker until he could not see the fir trees any more, but he knew they were only a few minutes walk. His excitement grew by each step, until his whole body seemed to tremble.

I wonder what the treasure is? Is it another magical symbol? I wonder how I'll know where to look for it?

He thought again of his best friend. *Oh Bobby how I wish you were here. You'd love this game.*

The wood grew denser and denser until the pathway and surroundings formed a kind of tunnel. Sam pushed on, his thoughts still on Bobby and their childhood treasure hunts.

*

It was Bobby's 11th birthday. His mum and dad had spent all day before setting up the most fantastic treasure hunt in the same wood. Screaming boys rushed around following the clues and gradually homing on in the ultimate prize. No one knew what the prize would be but they were promised it would be worth it. The winner turned out to be a boy called Freddy. He managed to crack the last cryptic message and dashed off to find his reward. The prize was as splendid as the hunt itself… it was a wooden chest containing a gift for each boy. The reward for young Freddy was not only to have one of the smaller gifts but also to be hero for the day, for his prize was also the prize of all the other boys in the party.

Sam always admired Bobby's parents for how fair there were. They knew how to treat their children and friends without spoiling them. They knew how to create fun and excitement without causing any rivalry or unhealthy competition.

*

The tunnel grew narrower and narrower. Sam pushed on occasionally looking down to make sure his feet were still on the path.

Gosh this is overgrown. It must be years since anyone's used this path?

Suddenly it seemed to get a little lighter. Though still dense and thick, ahead was a definite slither of daylight entering from the outside. Sam squeezed himself onwards and, there in the distance, he caught a glimpse of a man-made wooden object.

'That's it,' he said, trying to hold back the excitement.

The tunnel had almost closed up completely.

Come on Sam, one more push.

It was like trying to squeeze a cat through a mouse hole. He tried again. Suddenly there was a snap, and human noise, and the sound of ripping fabric.

'Aggggh!'

Sam sat up, and looked at his left coat sleeve. It was torn right up to the elbow. He looked back at the place he'd fallen through. *Gosh how the hell did I get through that?*

The hole in the bush had all but closed up again. Sam was still dazed from the fall and hadn't yet looked up at the object of his destination.

The colour ran from Sam's face as he heard someone say, 'Congratulations! You made it'.

'What?' The young man jumped to his feet and turned to face the Wizard, who was sat on the Reading Chair holding a small shovel in his hand. 'But how?'

'Not how but why?'

'No,' demanded Sam, 'come on you've got to tell me. How on earth did I end up back here?'

'Sam I promise you the question is not how but why. Why you got back

here is simply because you followed my instructions and didn't give up.
Your heart was strong Sam. You were led by your desire. That's why you
came back here. *How* you got back will forever remain a mystery.'

'I've never been more amazed by anything in my life. I just don't understand at all. What just happened is completely impossible.'

'Clearly it is not.'

'So the treasure. I take it there was none?'

'Sam there are two types of treasure, and both you will have experienced by the end of today.'

The Wizard held up the shovel.

'What do you want me to do with it?' asked Sam.

'What do you normally do with a shovel?'

'Dig!'

'And dig is what you must do now Sam. Dig for what I sent you to find.'

'Where do I dig?'

'Try right where you are now standing.'

There under Sam's feet was a definite patch of recently dug earth.

'It was here all along?'

'Yes, but the task was to go on a hunt. You would not be able to
comprehend the mystery of what lies beneath your feet had you not have
made today's journey.'

'That's why you gave me no spade or shovel'

'Precisely,' said the Wizard.

Sam had to dig down a foot and a half before hitting something wooden
and hollow. After carefully removing the last few shovel loads of earth he
reached down and brought out a small wooden chest. Once more Sam was
in awe. The box filled him with wonder. It was rectangular and made from
oak, but it had no lid or opening point.

'Come, bring it over here,' said the Wizard.

Sam carried the box and sat down next to the old man on the Reading
Chair. He placed the chest on his lap.

'How do I open it?' said Sam.

'That's for you to discover,' replied the Wizard smiling gently.

'You're loving every bit of this aren't you Mr. Wizard? Do you know how tired I am?'

'Of course, but I also know how much *you* are enjoying it. Right now you can't stop wondering what's inside can you?'

Sam studied the box but for the life him could not find any sign of a latch, or lid, or opening of any kind.

Then he remembered the Wizard's words: "The task was to go on a hunt. You would not be able to comprehend the mystery of what lies beneath your feet had not have made today's journey."

Something about today's hunt holds the key to opening this box.

'Come on Sam,' said the Wizard, '*See* the answer. Stop thinking so much and let it come... be open.'

'But I'm trying.'

'You are trying too hard. Relax and allow your subconscious mind to show you.'

Sam closed his eyes and tried to make himself relax but it was not easy. Suddenly a picture popped into his mind. He saw himself looking down at the map... but he saw something he hadn't registered before. *How odd!* He opened his eyes and took out the map again. Sure enough it was as the picture had just shown him: The Reading Chair / departure point had been marked very close to the left hand side of the map, and the destination point, with the four fir trees had been marked on the far right hand side. It hadn't occurred to Sam before because it just seemed like the map maker had needed as much space as possible to draw the whole thing.

I wonder, he thought as he rolled the map into a cylinder. The two sides came together and the start and end points of the journey met. Sam looked on the map in wonder. It was then that he noticed the words. Right along the point where the two sides of the page met were the distinct markings of words. Sam separated them again and the words seemed to disappear becoming just random markings that didn't resemble anything. Bringing them together again they definitely re-formed into a sentence.

'What is the gift of an unopened chest? Break to discover what you'll never recover.'

Sam looked at the Wizard, 'Do I have to smash it open? Is that what it's saying?'

'Sometimes things have to be broken to uncover the glories within Sam'

'Ok.'

Sam took the box and placed it down on the gravel path. He held the shovel high above the chest. It came down at speed, but stopped before it hit the box.

'Well done Sam,' said the Wizard.

'My God you were going to let me smash it!'

'But you didn't Sam.'

'No, but I was going to.'

'So what stopped you?'

'As I started to bring the shovel down over the box I suddenly realised what the saying meant. The value of this box is that it is unopened. It contains something precious but it's a mystery. If I were to open it it would no longer be a mystery. It would no longer be... magic. It might contain a precious jewel worth more than words could express. But it might just as well be empty, yet even empty it has a value when unopened because it contains a mystery. I am beginning to understand. I really am.'

'Good Sam, and you would never have uncovered that truth were it not for the journey. If you had just dug up the box at ten this morning you'd have spent all day trying to get in to it and finally smashed it open, losing the *real* treasure. Sam, this box is your third gift. Never open it. It will be a constant reminder that mystery is good. You sometimes think too much Sam. You try to analyse everything and have it all neatly worked out. Mystery is good. Mess and muddle is good. Let go of the need for answers to everything. Let go and live.'

'Thank you,' said Sam holding his mysterious prize with such tenderness.

'I think you ought to take your box and go home now Sam. We've got more to do tomorrow and I think you'll sleep even better tonight after all your walking. What I suggest is this; after supper have a hot bath and let your mind wander over what you've learned so far. Don't force your thinking too much. Just let your mind drift. Then go to bed and we'll meet again tomorrow.'

CHAPTER 42

Jane sat in the Reader's front room with her note pad in front of her. She was ready to ask her three questions.

'Now Jane,' said the woman, 'before we start again there's something I need to ask you.'

'Ask away.'

'It's not an easy question to ask.'

Jane looked concerned, 'What do you mean? What are you going to ask me?'

The Reader was sat on the other side of the room. It was a cosy room with a comfortable settee and dim lighting. She stood up and moved over to sit next to Jane.

'Jane,' she said, as she placed her hand on her forearm and looked into her eyes, 'if you had a chance to go back in time and get that job, the one you did your last presentation for, would you?'

'You mean my dream travel job?'

'Yes that's precisely what I mean.'

'What difference does it make now? I can't go back. That's a non question.'

'No Jane, it's a serious question, and one I do need to ask. Think carefully and try to answer me.'

Jane thought. She knew that if she were really able to go back to that point and get the job of her dreams she'd not be there with the Reader now. She'd know nothing of this whole episode with the cards or the readings. On the other hand she'd be set to travel and explore the world. She closed her eyes at the thought of it and the Reader could see a beautiful smile appear on the younger woman's face as she dreamed. But then the smile disappeared and Jane opened her eyes.

'No, no I would not go back. It would have been my dream, but now I am content to be here. If it meant having my dream but losing this experience then I would not want it.'

The Reader beamed and threw her arms round Jane. 'My dear,' she said, 'you are the most amazing young woman. Thank you for coming to me last Sunday. You've so touched my heart.'

'But why did you feel you had to ask me that?' said Jane.

'Because I needed to know how open I should be about where all this might lead for you. And now I know. I can be free to let you have it all.'

'I'm not sure I know what you mean.'

'Well, Jane you remember me alluding to the fact that the cards can't predict your future, and that I can't either?'

'Yes,' said Jane, 'In fact I was going to bring that up today.'

'You were?'

'Yes but please, go on. I'll ask you later.'

'Well,' continued the Reader, 'What I said was true, the future is not something these cards foretell, but sometimes, just every once in a while I do catch a glimpse of something that seems to be unfolding in one of my client's lives. I never speak much of this to my usual sitters because most of them only want cheap fortunes and I refuse to encourage that. But you are different, and I feel something is indeed coming for you. You are soon going to be given an opportunity to begin once more at something you've told yourself you'll never have again, only this time it will be real and true and long lasting. Does this mean anything to you Jane?'

Jane's eyes overflowed as she listened to the words of hope. She knew what the Reader was seeing even if the Reader herself was unclear.

'Yes, yes I know of whom you speak. I saw him today. He was my lover once but it all went wrong. I've never been able to trust anyone since. Maybe he's come back as my Wizard at the end of the road?'

'Jane,' the Reader looked cautious, 'I'm not saying I know what this is all about. I am just saying something is happening for you. But please be careful my dear. Just be careful… now let's look at the cards shall we?'

The two women studied and chatted and thought about the cards. Together they looked over all of Jane's notes so far.

I don't know what's happening but I know I need to write. I'm not even sure who I'm writing this for. I feel confused but excited. I've just watched a film that I've seen so many times. As a child I saw it every Christmas without fail, yet today it was not just a film, and not just a walk down memory lane. It rang bells... huge loud bells. A girl who finds herself on a journey she's not asked for; a girl who is given three strange new friends to travel with and learn from. A journey to find a powerful Wizard who himself turns out to be a frail little man. Four co-travellers with four individual .quests, each of them discovering that the very thing they thought they needed they actually possessed all along.

Am I Dorothy? I feel like I've been placed at the beginning of some yellow brick road myself. Was I meant to go to that psychic fayre? Was I even meant to screw up my presentation? I have so many questions. Why am I so excited by all this? I've never been into this kind of thing, not since my early teens. And what about the cards and the things I wrote only a couple of hours ago? Have I been caught up in some delusion or was that Reader-women for real? Are the cards she gave me really going to take me on a journey?

Card number 1 - The Controller. Perfection's futile dream; Through cracks true light will gleam.

A young man climbing a huge ladder, propped up against a tower. He is close to the top and looks unstable and fragile. There is a flock of birds but one bird is flying in the wrong direction. A dead bird lies on top of the tower. I think that the dead bird has been killed by the sun and the other bird is flying away from the sun. The man is climbing toward it/into it. It seems he has dropped a pot of gold dust. There is a small pile of yellow gold powder next to the broken pot as well as a scattering of it all down the rungs of the ladder.

My three cards. (left) The Controller, (centre) The Traveller, (right) True Love

First card turned - centre = the present. Subtext - The physical journey denied, a spiritual journey implied.

My notes: When plans to move are shattered a deeper force may be at work and more subtle inner movements of the soul may be taking place.

Lesson: Surrender to what is, and look for signs of growth, spiritual and emotional development.

Personal application: For whatever reason I was denied my dream of physical travel, but have been given an opportunity for a new spiritual and psychological journey. WOW.

Second card turned – left = The past / the character formed. The ego.

Subtext - Perfection's futile dream; Through cracks true light will gleam.

My notes: The hardest card to fully interpret. Much symbolism and detail. I see myself on that ladder, straining to climb and carrying the trophies of my success. Yet I also see that these trophies somehow need letting go of for their true glory to be revealed . . . the gold dust spilling out from the broken pot.

I know I am a control freak and perfectionist in every area of my life from work to relationships. The card seems to warn that such ambitious lifestyles can potentially lead to death – the dead bird frazzled by the hot sun.

The gold dust also paves the way for a journey... but it is a journey DOWN the ladder not UP higher. The truth is at the bottom. What truth is this?

Still much interpretation needed here... my thoughts continue.

Back to work today. Tough going. Heart not in it. Couldn't stop thinking of the cards all day.

I feel more and more that the card to the left is me. I am a controller. I have tried to control my life to the point where there is no room for spontaneity or fun. No room for error of failure. No room to enjoy life. In my pursuit of success I have failed at the game of life. But it's not too late. I do not need to end up a dead bird on a roof top. I need to find the gold that is at the bottom of the ladder. I'm not sure where to look but big changes are ahead. Excitement.

Still need help with this card. Will wait for Reader to advise. Now on to final card.

Third card turned – right = The future / unrealised potential and possibility. The True Self. True Love. Cling and you will kill, let go and you will keep, this is the purest love to seek.

At first this card angered me. My own pain of the pain. Abused trust. Broken promises. I was stabbed in the back by my first serious boyfriend. Love turned to hate. I still carry the wounds. I now see that the two souls in the picture have not wounded each other but bear the wounds of the past. Yet they have found healing by letting go of hatred and letting go of the need for possessive love. The two lovers can love because they are free and the space between them symbolises their ability to love without clinging... to possess love without being possessed by love.

Will I ever find this kind of love? God knows I long for it but all the men I've met since him have never coped with my coldness... the fact that I can't let them close in case they hurt me. Yet again I see myself as a controller.

Also a goal of a human life is to love Self.

Other features of the card: ripples in the pond, something golden and glowing in the centre of the pond beneath the water, the space between the two characters is a different colour to the rest of the card – a hazy blue colour. Not sure yet what any of these features represent.

Notes on Thursday - lunch break:

Today I am drawn to the gold glittering beneath the surface of the pond. What can it mean? My instincts tell me it speaks of a treasure yet to be discovered. It is a hidden treasure that exists within the space between two lovers. Gold seems to be everywhere. I am dreaming of following a yellow golden pathway to meet a Wizard. Gold is spilled down the ladder in the Controller card. Gold exists at the bottom of the ladder too...

The next few words stood out with coloured light as the two women read...

Oh my God. I've just seen it. I am to be given another chance. There *will* be another relationship for me, but the gold will not be locked away

inside him but between us, within our spaces as well as our being together. I put all my eggs in one basket before and when it fell apart protected myself by building a great wall and setting out to climb a huge ladder of perfection and success. The overseas job would have been the pathway to every success I dreamed of, yet inside I would have remained lonely for I was climbing away from myself. The cards were right. The traveller card spoke of a new beginning... a spiritual journey. I can now safely say I've accepted the journey even though I still do not know where it leads.

The controller card showed me who I was becoming but also that my salvation is not up there at the top, where the sun shines brightly (where the dead bird lies) but down at the bottom, where the cracked pot lies spilling out gold.

It's all tying together now. My God it seems Jenny Thrip had an important place in my life after all. I still wonder about this Wizard? Perhaps it's simply a dream, after all I'd reminded myself of my favourite childhood movie. It was bound to shows up in my dreams.

'Jane, when did you write this?' said the Reader.

'Er, yesterday, during my lunch break.'

'You have done so well my dear. I knew you had the gift. Your summary here is so close to what I have been feeling myself. But let's not be too hasty in our thoughts about this Dan. As I told you before these cards do not foretell events, they mirror the state of your soul and they awaken the things you need to learn. It's closer to what the psychologist Carl Jung called synchronicity than what psychics call fortune telling.'

'So do you think I should avoid Dan when he calls?'

'No my dear, for some reason he's shown up again, but it might be that he has something to teach you.'

Jane's complexion changed and her face darkened, 'Dan taught me never to trust another man.'

'Yet part of you now yearns for his touch.'

'Yes I was infatuated with him. I don't think I loved him. It was more like an addiction. I needed him and when he left it was like hell... I can't believe cold turkey's a fraction as painful as what I went through.'

'So seeing him has brought these memories to the foreground again?'

'Yes, I guess so,' said Jane.

The Reader reached out and picked up the True Love card. She held it so they could both look at it.

'Where is Dan in this picture Jane?'

Jane took the card from the older woman and held it close to her face. She gazed at it for a while and then turned to the Reader, her eyes looking as hollow as those of a pining dog.

'He's not there. I can't see him anywhere in this picture,'

'Jane, this is really important, I want you to look again and ask yourself where you'd place him if you could.'

'What, in the card?'

'Yes Jane.'

Suddenly she saw it. She knew exactly, 'There,' she said, and with a pointed forefinger jabbed a particular place on the card, 'right there, behind the woman. He's holding the bloody knife.'

*

'How can you say that to me?' cried a younger Jane, 'don't you love me anymore?'

'Look, you suffocating little girl, I'm going out and that's the last of it.'

'But it's my birthday!'

The broken young woman slid down the bathroom wall and landed in a crumpled heap at the bottom. It had been weeks since they'd had a night to themselves and, stupidly, she'd imagined a birthday dispensation from her bully of a lover. She'd been wrong.

'Give me one good reason why any man would want to spend an evening with a spoilt, whining wretch like you?' shouted Dan from the lobby.

Then, *slam*, he was gone.

Jane raised her head, her eyes stinging, 'Why? Why does he treat me like this?'

*

'He was a bastard,' said Jane, now sobbing as the painful memories flooded her mind. 'He was so cruel to me. He didn't care a damn how I felt. *I did love him.* I've been wearing a suit of armour since it all happened. I've even kidded myself into believing I never really cared about him. God he was my first *love* and my bloody last. Never again I said. Why did he have to show up and bring it all up again?'

'There's a reason why, Jane.'

'What reason?'

'Dan has reminded you of your buried pain and when we bury our pain it never goes away but just festers and grows and finds other ways of escaping, in damaging and unhealthy ways.'

'He's not come back for me has he?' said Jane.

'Jane my dear, I cannot answer that. I suspect even someone like Dan could have changed over the years you've been apart, but my caution with him is that going back is rarely a sensible choice. Rather I feel Dan is teaching you that you need to go forward and move on. The emotions you are now experiencing is all the pent up pain and anguish from the last few years of your life. You've been so good at bottling it up. But now the cork's come out and that needed to happen. Jane you will be able to move on now and I do think you will soon be ready for love again. You are young, beautiful and intelligent. All you need now is a little more love of Self.'

'Yes I wrote that too didn't I but ignored it when I re-read it today.'

'You did indeed Jane.'

'I guess Dan's not my Wizard of Oz then… the pot of gold at the end of my journey!' Jane looked at the woman, tears once more flooding down her cheeks, 'Is there a Mr Right for me, somewhere out there?'

The Reader looked with compassion at her young friend, 'My poor child. I bet you wish you still wore that suit of armour but Jane let me tell you something, the secret is not in searching for the right person but making yourself the right person. This is the paradox of love. There is no Mr Right or Mrs Right, yet on the other hand all are Mr Right and all are Mrs Right.'

'I don't understand.'

The Reader took the card from Jane and looked at it. 'You see that blue space between the two figures?'

Jane took a hanky out and blew her nose, 'Yes, I've written about that in my notes,'

'Well what's the colour we usually associate with love?'

'Red,' said Jane.

'Right, but red is only part of the love we need within relationships. The red fire of passion is powerful and exciting, but on its own leads to eventual suffocation and death.'

'Explain!'

'When all there is is passion based on lust then the relationship will go in one of two directions. The first is that when the red passion eventually fades for both of the lovers, then all they end up with is a pile of barely smouldering cinders marking the death of the union. When the passion fades for just one lover, the other will start to sense it and grow dependent. This dependence then manifests itself in clinginess, neediness and often jealousy and paranoia, which itself pushes the less dependent partner away even more. It becomes a vicious circle and is all too common.'

Jane knew exactly what the Reader meant, 'But what is this blue cloud in the picture then?'

'The gentle blue cloud represents true love which is not based on need or possessiveness but in giving and letting go. Blue is the colour of the spiritual world. The two lovers here are content because they have grieved over their wounds and learned to let go of the past. They are then capable of looking not to each other for their meaning but to themselves.'

'What do you think went wrong with me and Dan then? I can recognise so much of what you've been saying but why did it get like that?'

'I think what happened is that, soon after it all began with Dan, you started to use the language that so many lovers use, a language that talks of him fulfilling all your needs, being the One, a match made in heaven etc. Am I right?'

'Yes, but I don't understand what's so wrong with that. It's how it all felt. I wasn't making it up.'

'I know you weren't. And it's not wrong, in fact it's quite natural. But it can often lead to something quite unhealthy. If both lovers think they've found their answer to everything in the other partner it can turn into co-dependence and when something goes wrong then all hell lets loose. And when one lover only uses this language it creates misery for both. I guess you started to quickly feel very insecure with Dan?'

'Yes.'

'And I guess he would often get angry and say, "Give me some space"?'

'Yes'

'And his response would make you worse, and then your response to that would make him worse'

'Yes yes yes! Oh God will I ever be ready for another man?'

'Yes Jane, because now you know, and knowledge is the first step to transformation.'

*

The two women talked on until it was late. That night Jane was too tired to complete her journal. She felt as though she'd been through an emotional boxing match, yet she also felt a strange inner warmth, a tingling warmth of anticipation. She slept like a baby.

PART 7

'SATURDAY'

CHAPTER 43

My God, look at that! Sam stood at his window with the kaleidoscope to his eye. The sight was astonishing. *Coloured diamonds falling from heaven.* It was raining but, through the wonderful eyepiece, what would usually evoke feelings of melancholy brought pure delight.

As yet he hadn't allowed any other person to see his three gifts. His mother was the *last* person he would trust with them.

'Sam'

He could hear her now, 'Yes mother.'

'Sam, I need you to come down for a moment.'

'On my way.'

It was nearly nine thirty. He'd already had his breakfast after the luxuri-ously long lie in. The Wizard's prediction had been right... it was a wonderful night's sleep. But now Sam's peace and joy was about to be stolen. He reached the bottom of the stairs and recognised the voices coming from the front room immediately. *Shit what do they want?*

'Hello Sam,' said the Minister. He was one of three men standing in the front room.

'What are you doing here again?'

'Sam, don't be rude, they've come to help you,' said his mother looking up.

'She's right,' said one of the two elders, 'you need our help Sam.'

Sam ignored the remark and, looking directly into the Minister's eyes, said, 'I'm going back upstairs to change, after which I will leave to visit the only person who is *really* helping me right now. When I come down I'll expect you to be gone.'

'You can't throw us out,' said the Minister, 'We're you mother's guests and it's her house not yours.'

Sam looked at his mother. She sat near the fire place with her head looking into her lap.

'Sam,' she said without looking at him, 'we're all so worried about you. Please let them pray with you at least.'

'You're not worried about me, any of you. You just care about the damn Fellowship and I've had enough of it.' He reached into the neck part of his dressing gown and grasped hold of something. 'I rid myself of the lot of you,' he shouted, as he threw his baptismal medallion to the floor. Then he walked out of the room and back upstairs.

Minutes later he was down again, tucking his shirt in as he walked. He grabbed his coat and slammed the front door behind him. The men were still there.

God I am beginning to hate them.

He turned the key, switched the wipers on, revved loudly and screeched off in the rain.

*

The Wizard sat waiting for Sam under the shelter of the Reading Chair roof as the angry young man stormed up the path toward him. He looked down at the floor as he walked, not lifting his head until he stood in front of his mentor. His face still bore the anger of his morning encounter with the three men.

'What is it?' asked the Wizard, his amber eyes displaying a subtle tenderness, 'sit down here and tell me what happened.'

'Those bastards,' said Sam, almost spitting as he spoke. 'They think they can control every part of my life.'

'I take it you mean the fellowship?'

'Damn right I do, and especially that bloody self-righteous Minister.'

'Sam I *do* know how you feel… more than you realise, but you mustn't let them take away your peace.'

The younger man held his heavy head in his hands and sighed, 'They make me mad. I feel so unworthy when they speak to me… so guilty. Over the last few years my own common sense has corrected some of the crap they've fed me but...'

'But what Sam?'

'But they still have power over me. I guess part of me still believes they are who they think they are.'

'And who's that?'

'The truth. They think they represent the ultimate truth about bloody everything.'

The old man reached out and placed his hand on Sam's shoulder and they sat like that for some time. Sam's mind whirled away like a camcorder on fast forward. He watched as hundreds of scenes passed by. Every so often he pressed the imaginary play button and watched the scene slow down. Ugly scenes. Painful memories. Dark times of confusion and guilt and in the centre of each scene... the Minister.

*

'*No Samuel*,' shouted the Minister to a youth of sixteen, 'you are wrong. There are *no* contradictions in God's Word.'

The occasion was a fellowship youth study night and it was Sam's turn to read from the scriptures. Each week a different young person would get to read a favourite passage, Old Testament or New, and then the Minister, or another Elder, would comment on it to the group. This particular night Sam had chosen a passage that, privately, had caused him much confusion. It was regarding the death of Judas, a character whom Sam has always felt more than a wave of sympathy for, though he knew better than to admit it. Through his own private readings Sam had unwittingly stumbled across a well known biblical problem - how and where did Judas die, for there seemed to be two highly different accounts?

Sam had read one of them as his chosen passage but, before allowing the Minister to comment, had asked the question about the apparent discrepancies. It was all too much for the Minister. It was not the place of any student to make any comments on the Scriptures let alone suggest there may be a question over how they do or don't harmonise.

'And in the company of your fellows Samuel! What if your reckless questions were to rock a brother's faith? I'll tell you What! *"If anyone causes the downfall of one of these little ones who believe, it would be better for him to be cast into the sea with a millstone round his neck."'* The Minister used short bible quotes like a gun in his hand.

From that day Sam chose not to publicly question anything again, but the confusion had never left his head never ceased.

*

'My dear Sam,' said the Wizard, still comforting him with his hand, 'I think it's rather good that today you come with all this turmoil and confusion.'

The young man lowered his hands and turned towards the Wizard, 'Good? How can it be good?'

The Wizard's face glowed and, though the day was cloudy and wet, his eyes sparkled brightly. He put his hand in his coat pocket and pulled out a book. 'Here, take this.'

'What is it?' asked Sam.

The book wore the hallmarks of being well read. A few pages were loose and the cover had been clearly replaced with a piece of soft hide. Written on the front, in faded golden calligraphy, were the words God Calling.

'It's a spiritual jewel,' said the Wizard, 'written back in the thirties by two anonymous women who we now know as the "Two Listeners". They claimed to have been given a series of mystical messages from Christ, profoundly wise messages that bring love, hope and comfort to those who read them. All we really know about them is that they were poor, sick and disillusioned, yet they found peace and joy from words they were given. Sam, I *know* they will do the same for you if you read them with an open mind. Your Christ, the one you've tried to serve all you life, yet feel constantly alienated from because of the fellowship's harsh teaching, will speak to you and transform your spiritual understanding of your God and of yourself.'

Sam looked down at the book in his hands. He carefully turned over the front cover. There was an inscription inside, *To Sam, with brightest blessings and warmest wishes. That's odd! Someone else called Sam has owned it.* He looked up at the Wizard, puzzled.

'What is it Sam?'

'Oh… nothing,' he said, and then added, 'you say it was written by two women who heard God's voice. The fellowship would have a thing to say about that.'

'Sam, this is going to take a real act of faith on your part for I cannot comment on the authenticity of this book. If you were to show it to your Elders I'm sure they'd take it to burn, but doesn't that make you just a little bit inquisitive?'

'Yes it does, and nervous too.'

'All I can say is that I received it when I was a younger man when I too was going through the same kind of inner debates that you are. I was sceptical when I first received it, but after spending some time with it I knew, *I just knew it spoke wisdom*. I don't know whether these women heard God's voice or whether they were somehow opened up to their own inner wisdom, but it is an *inspiration*. Millions have found it so.'

'Millions? Why haven't I heard of it before?'

'Why would you? And if you had it would more than likely be as a book to avoid. My suggestion for today Sam, is that you find a place to sit and read… and when you want to, come back and let me know your thoughts.'

Sam struggled. His two voices were having their own debate:

What harm can it do?

Are you kidding? Harm. It's obviously error. Remember what it says at the end of Revelation?

But the Wizard. He's shared so much. He's given me so much. I've grown to trust him. He might be right about it?

Sam… Sam…Sa

Quiet. I'm going to give it a chance.

Sam looked once more at the Wizard, who was smiling. 'Ok.'

'There's just one thing to point out Sam,' said the Wizard, 'it was written in the form of daily passages. Bear that in mind as you read. Read them slowly, do not try to take in too much too soon. I just want you to get a taste of what it contains?

CHAPTER 44

Jane had been in a dream all morning. She still was when he walked in.

'Hello beautiful,' he said, as he leaned over the cosmetic counter and flashed a wide smile at her, 'sorry, did I startle you?'

'Dan!' she said, blinking her eyes rapidly in an effort to wake herself up. 'I didn't see you come in.'

'You were *on the moon* Jane. My hunch is you were thinking about our date!'

She grabbed the edge of the counter to steady herself before the giddiness could send her to the floor with a crash. *God am I going to faint?*

'Jane, are you ok?' he said, 'you look... pale. Is something wrong?'

'Dan,' said Jane taking a breath, 'I'm afraid there's not going to be a date, at least not for a while. I'm ok. Really. I've just had a lot on lately and... I'm sorry but I can't meet you.'

'I see,' he said, his smile now all but gone, 'but I thought we could...'

'It's too complicated. I know you're only asking me for a meal and a catch up but you know what might happen.'

'Exactly!' he said half-smiling again.

'No! We were wrong before and I have no reason to think it'll be any different now... do I? Dan do you know how much pain our relationship caused me?'

'I've changed.'

'So have I Dan. So have I.'

Dan turned and walked back out of the shop.

Jane watched him and lifted a finger to wipe the tear from her cheek.

CHAPTER 45

'What's the matter?' asked the Wizard who watched the young man walk slowly up the path towards him.

Sam moved like a sleep walker. He seemed to be in a dream. His zombie-like eyes were red and watery and he rocked from side-to-side as he walked. He'd been gone for about three hours. He said nothing as he approached.

'Sam! Talk to me!' demanded the old man.

At this point he looked up and, wearing a look of complete bewilderment, said, 'Ok I believe you. You were right about this.' He held up the leather bound book nodding to it with his head.

The Wizard breathed, 'Sam isn't it beautiful?'

Sam looked dazed. What he'd experienced over the last few hours had profoundly affected him. Anyone apart from the Wizard would have sworn he'd smoked a joint.

He sat down next to his mentor, 'I've never read anything like it in my life.'

'I felt the same, the first time I read it Sam. In fact I would say it *changed* my life.'

'I don't know why but it rang so many bells for me. It was like everything I have wanted to express about just about everything, God, love, faith, Jesus, myself . . . !' He shook his head, 'I just couldn't believe I was reading it.'

Suddenly the Wizard looked serious. 'Sam, you know what they will say if they find this?'

'Who? The fellowship?'

'Yes, *and* your mother.'

'Well they won't find it. None of them will.'

Sam held the book to his heart. *Thank you, God. Thank you for speaking to me. Thank you for giving me this.*

'Tell me then Sam. Tell me what it felt like as you read.'

He looked directly into the Wizard's eyes, 'Its words sounded familiar - this voice of Christ. It was as though I'd heard it before.'

'You have,' said the Wizard, 'many times throughout your life.'

'But the only Christ I've heard about has been through the fellowship, and his voice is not like this.' He held up the book and pointed to it with his other hand. 'The Christ I hear preached can be so frightening, and has always made me feel that I have something missing – that I'm not enough in myself – that I have to prove myself... Yet these words, though so challenging, do not threaten or judge. They are kind, gentle and loving. They are certainly not easy to follow for they speak of a way of life that is almost alien to my ways, a way of loving without fear, without paranoia, with no future dreads, no regrets of past mistakes. But for the first time in my life a spiritual book has made me feel special rather than unworthy.'

'Sam the voice is the wisdom that lives inside all people. That's why you've heard it before. That's why it sounded so familiar. The problem is that so few of us ever stop to listen to it.'

'Is it the voice you told me to listen to when you talked about the suffo-cating ivy? You said it was "quieter, calmer, unflustered and unconfused?"'

'In a way yes, but Sam there is a deeper voice still... which is the voice of the purest wisdom.'

'*Another* voice?'

The Wizard stood up and turned to face Sam. He reached out his arms and held them wide apart. Sam looked up with wide eyes.

'Sam, *this* is your confused voice.' He turned his left hand face up and nodded to it with his head. 'It is part of you and not to be avoided but often its tone is negative and angry. It is angry because of fear. It is one side of the conversation that you have almost constantly in your mind. *This* is your quieter calmer voice.' He motioned the same way with his right hand. 'It is the voice of clarity - the other half of the conversation. It is usually more trustworthy than the other voice but you need both in order to make your way through life. If you didn't have this inner debate you would not experience half the glory available.'

Sam looked confused, 'I don't understand.'

The Wizard lowered his arms for a moment. 'Let me put it this way. If there was no battle there would be no struggle and if there was no struggle there would be no growth and therefore no enlightenment.'

'Explain.'

'You'd never know the liberation of a truly free mind were you not also prone to a bound up mind. You'd never know the beauty of peace were it not for the reality of confusion.'

'Ok, I see. But you also spoke of another voice - a voice of even deeper wisdom.'

'I'm coming to that now Sam. Let me ask you can you remember hearing those two voices recently?'

'Of course, they are nearly always there, and sometimes they argue so loudly that it clutters my whole mind. It feels like there are two people inside me.'

'Look,' said the Wizard, raising his arms again, 'here are your two voices. Am I right that sometimes *this one* wins,' he wiggled his left hand, 'and off you go into an eventual pit of despair?'

'Yes,' said Sam.

'And sometimes *this one* wins,' the Wizard wiggled his right hand, 'and you find you have peace of mind?'

'Yes, that's right but usually *that* one wins,' said Sam, pointing at the Wizard's left hand, 'though over the last few days the other voice has been much stronger. In fact my confused mind has become much less of a problem.'

'Ok, we're getting somewhere. Now can you answer me, what is it that has made you listen to your calmer voice these last few days?'

'You Mr. Wizard. You told me to.'

'But I haven't been with you all the time have I.'

'No, but I can hear you guiding me and saying 'Sam, remember to listen to the quieter voice.'

'Sam, look now.' The Wizard still held out his two arms but now nodded his head and faced Sam directly. 'Here is the third voice. It is the voice that reminds you which of the other two to listen to.'

Sam stood up as if his chair had become electric. 'Oh my God,' he said, 'Yes I do understand. I really do. I've always had that inner argument as you call it, but I've heard that third voice over these last few days. It's like *you* are whispering in my mind.'

The Wizard put his arms down, 'That's only because I have become your teacher Sam and you associate my voice with the voice of wisdom.'

'This is remarkable. How do I allow that voice more space in my head?'

'Over time, Sam, that inner guide will become much more evident for you. Take the four gifts I've given you and use them. They will all contribute to this. Today's gift *is* a book that was written entirely from the perspective of that voice, which is why it sounded so familiar to you, as it does to all who read it.'

'I couldn't believe it,' said Sam, 'reading those words was like reading something I already knew yet didn't.'

The Wizard sat down and patted the seat next to him for Sam to join him. 'Let's look at the book together for a while. I'll show some passages that will remind you of the first three gifts.'

The two men sat and thumbed their way through the leather bound book filling their minds with wonderful sayings about the beauty of the present moment, the elimination of fear and the need for mystery and magic. The Wizard showed Sam the following four passages:

Seek Beauty
Draw Beauty from every flower and Joy from the song of the birds, and the colour of the flowers.

Drink in the beauty of air and colour. I am with you. When I wanted to express a beautiful thought, I made a lovely flower. I have told you. Reflect.

When I want to express to man what I am - what my Father is - I strive to make a very beautiful character.

Think of yourselves as My expression of attributes, as a lovely flower is My expression of thought, and you will strive in all, in Spiritual beauty, in Thought - power, in Health, in clothing, to be as fit an expression for Me as you can.

Absorb beauty. As soon as the beauty of a flower or a tree is impressed upon your soul it leaves an image there which reflects through your actions. Remember that no thought of sin and suffering, of the approaching scorn and Crucifixion, ever prevented My seeing the beauty of the flowers.

Look for beauty and joy in the world around. Look at a flower until its beauty becomes part of your very soul. It will be given back to the world again by you in the form of a smile or a loving word or a kind thought or a prayer.

Listen to a bird. Take the song as a message from My Father. Let it sink into your soul. That too will be given back to the world in ways I have said. Laugh more, laugh often. Love more. I am with you. I am your Lord.

"The heavens declare the glory of God; and the firmament sheweth his handiwork." - Psalm 19:1

Follow Your Guide

I am with you to guide you and help you. Unseen forces are controlling your destiny. Your petty fears are groundless.

What of a man walking through a glorious glade who fretted because ahead there lay a river and he might not be able to cross it, when all the time, that river was spanned by a bridge? And what if that man had a friend who knew the way - had planned it - and assured him that at no part of the journey would any unforeseen contingency arise, and that all was well?

So leave your foolish fears, and follow Me, your Guide, and determinedly refuse to consider the problems of tomorrow. My message to you is, trust, and wait.

"I will instruct thee and teach thee in the way which thou shalt go: I will guide thee with mine eye." - Psalm 32:8

Mysteries

Your Hope is in the Lord. More and more set your hopes on Me. Know that whatever the future may hold it will hold more and more of Me. It cannot but be glad and full of Joy. So in Heaven, or on earth, wherever you may be, your way must be truly one of delight.

Do not try to find answers to the mysteries of the world. Learn to know Me more and more, and in that Knowledge you will have all the answers you need here, and when you see Me Face to Face, in that purely Spiritual world, you will find no need to ask. There again all your answers will be in Me.

Remember, I was the answer in time to all man's questions about My Father and His Laws. Know no theology. Know Me. I was the Word of God. All you need to know about God you know in Me. If a man knows me not, all your explanations will fall on an unresponsive heart.

Why art thou cast down, O my soul? and why art thou disquieted within

*me? Hope in God; for I shall yet praise him, who is the health of my
countenance, and my God. Psalm 43:5*

The Voice Divine

The Divine Voice is not always expressed in words.

It is made known as a heart-consciousness.

"Be still, and know that I am God." Psalm 46:10

'This book is profound,' said Sam, 'It's what I've needed for so long. These
women followed the Saviour and spoke His words didn't they!'

'They spoke the words of the cosmic Christ Sam, the universal divine
voice... the voice of wisdom that has been known through many spiritual
paths and traditions.'

'They were Christians though?'

'Yes Sam, they were. I've told you that, but not only Christians find
their words comforting. Their words are more universal that even they
themselves would have been aware of.'

'They have given the world a beautiful gift. I wonder why it came
through them?'

'These two women,' said the Wizard, holding the now closed book in
his hand, 'knew from their own broken lives how to get to this inner
wisdom. Their pain, rather than something to be bitter about, was used as
an opening point for magic. It is often when we are wounded that we
become closer to the inner voice.'

'But it's not just when we're broken that we hear it?'

'No Sam, it's also when we stop! There is so little space for wisdom in
the modern world. But spending time in the present moment and allowing
everything to slow down to the here and now... well, that it where the
wisdom speaks, because that is the only place of true reality. These two

listeners were able to write these wonders because they did not run away from the present, which is what most would have done in their situation. Many would have sunk into addiction or just wished their lives away but the two listeners stayed with their painful present and became open to the treasure that was right there with them.'

'Thank God for them. They left us with a remarkable book,' said Sam taking it from the Wizard and opening it again, 'I will treasure it forever.'

'I know you will Sam, and tomorrow you will be given a treasure that you do not have to carry in your hand at all.'

Sam's eyes opened wide, 'The fifth gift?'

'Yes,' replied the Wizard, 'but *stay in today* and enjoy this jewel. Tomorrow will come when it's ready.'

CHAPTER 46

'Hello Jane'

'Thank God, you're in. Is there any way we can meet tonight? I've just got in from work and I *really* need to talk to you.'

'My dear I'm with someone tonight. I'm so sorry but look, tomorrow's Sunday. Why don't you come over in the morning?'

'Ok. Thank you. I'll call at about nine then, if that's ok.'

'That'll be fine my dear.'

CHAPTER 47

'Sam, I don't want to talk about this morning. I'm just glad you're safely home and didn't try to do anything silly again. I could see how angry you were.'

'Then let's not spoil our meal by bringing it up mother. Ok.'

The two of them, mother and son, sat at the dinner table. It had been a pleasant evening. Sam had come home in a much brighter mood than when he left and his mother had tried to make it up by cooking him a real treat for dinner. It was now around nine pm and Sam was itching to get up to his room so he could read from his book.

'Tell you what son. I'll make you a nice mug of chocolate, just like I used to make them. Would you like that?' She knew he would.

'Thank you mother.'

She left the table and, a few minutes later, returned with a steaming mug of creamy chocolate. 'There you go, why don't you take that up with you and have a good night's sleep. I'll see you in the morning.'

'I will,' said Sam, 'bringing the mug to his lips. 'Mmm, just like I remember. In fact, even better.' The taste was heavenly and, perhaps because he hadn't had this favourite drink for so long, he even had a little head rush.

'Take it upstairs then my son. Night'

PART 8

'SUNDAY'

CHAPTER 48

Jane drove the usual route. It was nearly nine am. *What's that?* She noticed something odd. *That's the flower guy... God, what's he been up to?*

She drove on a few yards and pulled up getting a clear view from the rear mirror. The other car drove off quickly, passing Jane and turning an immediate left. Something felt wrong. What she saw didn't ring true. Her instincts told her to follow. She obeyed.

*

'I'm so sorry I'm late,' said Jane as she made her way into the Reader's front room.

'My dear! You look flustered. What is it? I'm sorry I couldn't see you last night. If I'd have known you were so...'

'No, it's not that.' Jane was shaking. 'I've just seen something really strange and I don't know what to do.'

'Tell me Jane. What did you see?'

'It was about half an hour ago. I was just arriving when I saw a car parked outside the house of someone I know. I glanced in as I drove past and someone was asleep in the passenger seat. It looked like there was another person in the back, a woman I think. The guy in the front looked just like a man I walked into on the street the other day. I stopped ahead and when I looked in the rear view mirror, two men in suits got into the car and drove off. It just didn't seem right.'

'Ok. So *then* what did you do?'

Jane looked like a guilty child, 'I followed the car.'

'Oh Jane you should have called the Police if you thought something was wrong.'

'I know but...'

'Never mind now. Come on what happened? Where did they go?'

'Funny thing is they drove to a strange religious looking building. Not one I've ever noticed before. I parked a little way away and watched. The man in the back got out and entered the building, only to return with another guy. They walked the half-asleep man into the building. It all seemed so weird but I felt better that it was clearly a religious thing.'

'And then you came here?'

'Yes,' said Jane, 'What do you think?'

'I think we should go and check this out. What's the man's name?'

'Sam,' said Jane.

CHAPTER 49

'Uggggh!'

   'Sam!'

   'Oougggh, I feel sick'.

   Sam's mother held her son's hand. 'I'm so sorry,' she said, 'but I had to.'

   'His eyes opened slightly but closed again as the painful light shot it, 'Aggggh. It burns.'

   'Oh Sam.'

   He tried to open them again, ever so slightly. 'My God where the hell am I?' The room was small and sterile. He could feel the hard rubber of the counselling couch under his head. He lifted it slightly and saw a modern painting on the wall opposite... a *religious* painting. There was the sound of muffled music coming from somewhere. His sight began to clear and he recognised the work of art, 'Oh shit, I know where I am.'

   'Sam forgive me.'

   'You bitch. What have you done. That bloody hot chocolate. No.' He looked at his watch but couldn't see what it said. 'What time is it?'

   'Nearly ten thirty', said a loud male voice from the other side of the room.'

   'Ten thirty! No I've got to get... I'm going to miss him.'

   'You already have!' said the Minister.

CHAPTER 50

The two women drew near to the building. This time the place looked busier to Jane. There were folk walking in through the front doors and the faint sound of worship music could be heard.

'Come on Jane, let's just join the crowd and see what it's all about.'

Jane noticed a sign. 'Look at that,' she said, pointing to the big bold words *10.30 am Worship Service - We welcome visitors*

'I guess it's ok to go in then,' said the Reader.

They were met by a young woman with a smile like the Cheshire Cat. 'Welcome,' she said thrusting a leaflet in their hands as they passed, 'Do go ahead and take a seat. There are still plenty of places.'

The women agreed to sit it out and keep alert. If they hadn't seen anything of the man by the time the service was over they'd find who ever was in charge and confront him.

CHAPTER 51

'Let me go' cried Sam. His hands were tied by his side. 'Please, today is my last meeting. I can't afford to miss it.'

'Be quiet Sam,' said the Minister, as he left the room.

'It's for the best Sam,' said his mother.

Sam turned his face toward her. He narrowed his eyes and pursed his lips. 'You are not my mother.'

CHAPTER 52

'What do we do now then?' said Jane as the Minister and elders left the platform signalling the Service's end?

'We'll accept the Leader guy's invitation for refreshments and opportunity for questions and ask him directly about the man you saw.'

'Ok let's do it,' said Jane.

They followed the other newcomers into a large room. The Minister was standing near a table with paper cups filled with fruit juice. He was talking to a young couple. The two women watched and waited until at last he was free.

'Let *me* do the talking,' whispered the Reader in Jane's ear and then said in a louder voice, 'excuse me.'

The man turned round. He looked formidable in his dark suit and tie. 'How can I help?' he said.

'You can help by answering us a question. What did you do with our friend Sam?'

Jane was surprised by the up front assertiveness of the Reader's question. The Minister looked shocked, but quickly lowered his raised eyebrows and formed a smile.

'I saw him being taken here this morning,' added Jane, not wanting to let the man think he could lie.

'If you really know Sam, and if you are his true friends, then you'll understand why here's here. He is sick and he needs help. He's here with us for protection.'

'Then can we see him?' said Jane.

The Minister thought for a moment.

So did Jane, *he knows damn well that if he doesn't let us see him we'll be back later with the bloody Police.*

'Ok, stay here for a moment. Take a seat. I'll go and tell his mother that someone wants to see her son.'

The Reader waited until he had gone, 'Mother? Jane what's this about a mother? Surly if his mother's with him he'll be ok!'

Jane was surprised by this too. *Oh she must have been the woman in the back of the car, but why?* She looked at the Reader held out her hands and shook her head.

CHAPTER 53

'Someone wants to see you Sam?' said the Minister as he stepped through the door with another Elder.

'Who?' said Sam lifting his head up as far as he could.

'Two women who say they are your friends. One of them is about your age and the other's a lot older. Who are they Sam? Are they part of your new circle of 'friends'. The older one looks like a Witch to me.'

Sam's head was still spinning from the powder his mother had slipped in his chocolate. But this news of two female friends made his head swim even more. *Who could they be? Am I dreaming again?*

'We'd better untie him,' said the Minister to Sam's mother, 'and let's keep to the same story. He got himself high last night and you requested we bring him here to the fellowship for prayer because he'd threatened to kill himself.'

Sam's mother looked at the Minister with astonishment. 'But that's a lie?' she said, confused.

'Look, it's not far from the truth,' he said, 'come on. Whatever happens the fellowship's got to stick together.'

'Bloody hypocrites! You're all bloody hypocrites, said Sam.

'Ok. Go and fetch them,' said the Minister to the elder, 'I'll stay here with Sam.'

The Minister untied Sam's hands and lifted the back of the couch so he could sit up. The feeling of being raised up made him feel quite giddy. He let his head flop back and thought of the Wizard. *Will I ever see you again?* He felt frightened and lonely. *Why did they do this? I was going to get my final gift today. Why?* He tried to comfort himself by bringing back all the events of the previous four days, but it was hopeless. Huge tears ran down the sides of his face onto his shirt. He couldn't be bothered to wipe them away.

My poor boy, said his mother to herself, *what did I allow them to do?*

And what have I done?

Suddenly there was a noise outside.

'Sam!' Jane threw open the door.

'What? Heck, Jane. What on earth are you doing here?'

'I drove past your house this morning and saw you being taken here. Are you ok? The Minister said you tried to commit suicide and that you needed their protection? Is he telling the truth?'

'Um, yes. Well about the suicide anyway, though it was a whole week ago. But no I don't need *their* bloody protection. I didn't ask to come here. They… she.' He stretched a finger out towards his mother and looked at her in disgust, 'she drugged me last night.'

'It's a lie, he got himself drunk again,' said the Minister.

'Stop it,' screamed Sam's mother, 'I can't take this.' She turned to Jane and, through tears of guilt said, 'My son's telling the truth. I made him sleep so the elders could bring him here and stop him going back to the forest. He's been meeting a man up there. A man we think is dangerous. At least, I *thought* he was.'

'Thought?' snapped the Minister, 'What do you mean thought?'

She turned to the man that she'd followed for the last few decades of her life. 'My son tried to kill himself a week ago. Since then he's been meeting a man. A man I know nothing about. But he's come back happier and more at peace than I've ever known. And you! You surprised me today when you lied.' She looked to the floor and sobbed. The Reader walked over to her and put her hand on her shoulder to comfort her.

'But it's too late now,' said Sam. I was due to meet him for the last time this morning at ten. My condition for receiving five gifts of wisdom was to be there at ten for five consecutive days. The bloody fellowship have won. They always do.

'Yes we do,' said the Minister smugly.

Then the Reader spoke, 'Sam, you don't know me. I'm a friend of Jane's. Can I suggest something?'

Sam looked at her like a jackpot winner who'd lost his lotto ticket, 'Ok,' he said, 'What?'

'Let *us* take you once more to the forest. I have no idea what's been going on. I have no idea of what you will find if you go there again, but your soul is crying loudly. I can hear it.'

*

Ten minutes later Jane's car drove in the direction of the forest. Sam sat next to her in the passenger seat, while the Reader and his mother occupied the back.

'I'd tell you all about last week's conversations Jane, but I'm afraid you'd think I was mad.'

'Oh I wouldn't be so sure of that,' replied Jane looking in the rear view mirror and winking at the Reader behind.

'When we get there, I'll go to the place where we usually meet. Will you wait for me?'

'Of course Sam,' said Jane.

'It's going to be past one o'clock though. That's over three hours late so I really don't expect...'

'Shhh,' said the Reader, 'Don't give up hope my dear.'

*

Finally the car swung into the park and Sam left the three women as he walked the familiar path to the Reading Chair.

He won't be there you fool.

Yes he will. He's too good a person to just leave you without finishing what he began.

Crap! He gave you his rules and you broke them.

But he's wise. He's a Wizard. He'll know it wasn't my fault.

He arrived. He looked up. He saw the Reading Chair. There was no Wizard.

See you were too bloody late!

'Noooooooooooo!'

CHAPTER 54

'What was that?' said Jane.

'What was what?' replied the Reader.

'I heard something, something like a scream. It was very faint but I'm certain it came from up in the woods.'

'Oh God,' panicked Sam's mother.

'Come on let's go' said Jane.

The three women got out of the car and slammed the doors. Jane pointed a hard plastic key fob at the car and the doors locked automatically. Together they rushed into the woods and looked for signs to the Reading Chair.

CHAPTER 55

Sam sat weeping on the floor, his knees drawn up close to his body and his arms wrapped around his legs. He held them tight and rocked back and forth. *Those bastards. They've ruined everything.*

Then he heard the voice, 'Sam.'

He shot up to his feet and looked around. 'Where are you?' He could hear him but he couldn't see him.

'Sam, look under the chair.' The words seemed to be coming from inside his head, yet it was the familiar voice of the Wizard.

With excitement bubbling up inside Sam dived under the Reading Chair and peered into the dark emptiness. Then he saw it, a cloth bag hanging from one of the wooden slats in the centre of the space. He grabbed the bag and crawled out.

What's this then?

He sat on the ground and tipped out two things; a small envelope with an inscription *'To Sam'*, and a purple velvet bag with something inside. Sam was intrigued. He decided to open the envelope first and, after doing so, unfolded the letter.

Dear Sam, you are about to discover the gift of all gifts.

Inside the velvet bag is your final prize.

Even if you were to lose the first four gifts, the truths they contain will be yours eternally once you've learned the secret of the fifth.

You will know also that I am with you always. I walk with you in the dark and in the light. My voice will ever be available to you.

Now open the bag and see, see, see...

Your Wizard (within)

'Wow,' Sam said, as he placed his hand into the bag and took out a looking glass. He almost didn't want to look. His heart thumped inside his chest like an African drum. Finally he tuned the mirror to face him and peered into it.

'Oh my God, it's you,' he said.

He sat gazing into the mirror facing the Wizard. Then gradually, like the metamorphosis of a TV Time Lord, the image began to grow younger and change. The bone structure remained the same but the deep lines faded, the sagging cheeks tightened, the grey darkened and the beard vanished. At last Sam saw his own reflection yet his eyes were sparkling brightly, like a large amber ring in the sunlight.

'I am the Wizard?'

Yes, Sam, said a voice from deep within, *you are.*

Just then Jane arrived. Sam looked up at them his eyes full of tears, yet shining like orange-golden lamps.

'Was he here?' said Jane, 'I heard something. That's why we came. The others are just a bit behind me.'

'Yes he was here, and he still is,' said Sam still shell shocked by the experience.

'Where is he then?'

Sam got up and walked over to her carrying the precious mirror. 'I am him, I am the Wizard Jane. I am the Wizard.'

'The Wizard? You? Oh my God!'

EPILOGUE

THE ENCHANTED FOREST

Be still!

Listen!

Can you hear him?

Stop for a moment... close your eyes... be here NOW!

Are you aware?

There is a forest... an ancient wood... a scary sacred place *in you.*

It can seem like an overgrown jungle of thoughts - densely compacted trees and bushes smothered in twisted vines and creepers.

These are the intertwined confusions of memories, assumptions, fears, beliefs, prejudices, judgements, failures and successes.

They are the many layers of ego clothing we've dressed in over the years. They form the background noise of our mind. Sometimes they are quieter, but sometimes they deafen us, ruling out any clarity of vision.

Stop!

Be still!

Be here NOW!

Notice the voices blowing like wind through the trees...

Be aware of the echoes of arguments, unfinished plans, inner dialogues of confusion, and the incessant demands of the inner critic.

Notice them and then *notice* that *you* are noticing them.

See, they are NOT you. They are just remnants of past experiences and dreams of future hopes...

Be still!

Be here NOW where neither past nor future exist and then you will be ready to meet him.

Meet who?

There is an inhabitant within this scary sacred wood - a dweller who is real. Someone lives here whose presence transforms it from a frightening jungle to an enchanted forest.

He is quiet... he waits for you to stop and come to him.

He is not forceful.

He stands with lamp in hand, there in the deepest, darkest heart of the forest.

He is the wise One...

The true inner guide...

The divine voice...

The higher Self...

He is the *Wizard Within*.

POSTSCRIPT

THE WIZARD WITHIN

There seems to be a desperate longing for inner peace and contentment in today's fast paced world. Just take a look in your local bookstore. Go to the areas marked Mind-Body-Spirit, Popular Psychology and Comparative Religion and see how many titles you can find that are written from this perspective. It seems like we in the West are more *rest-less* than ever. Perhaps we've lost something? Perhaps we've become disconnected from something that was once a natural part of life. This is just my opinion of course, but I believe we have become almost immune to the sound of our inner wisdom – what I call the *Wizard Within*. It is the deepest magic that exists at the centre of the forest of our thoughts... underneath all the inter-twined creepers and vines. I believe that all of us have this Wise One inside us, but that his or her words have become drowned out by the background noise of our modern lives.

I became aware of the *Wizard Within* a few years ago after I decided to re-read my spiritual journal. I'd been keeping one for about twenty years, a simple ring binder with some paper. It was full of all my thoughts and experiences that have been spiritually interesting – lessons learned from high points and lows. When I re-read it I had a big surprise for I started to detect a strange pattern in my notes. One-half of the pattern was an obsessive feeling of unworthiness and perfectionism, expressed through written rituals of repentance - pledges and promises to God saying 'this time I'll be better' etc. The journal contained evidence that its author felt really bad about himself. I was like millions of other 'success orientated' Westerners who've sadly ended up feeling inadequate, unworthy, and basically not good enough. But I was a *Christian* when I wrote this stuff! Why would a Christian become so tormented by self-hatred? Well simple really. I was doing what many Christians do [and I imagine we are not alone]; I was projecting my own false images onto God. I was mentally creating a *God* in the image and likeness *of human beings* rather than the other way round. When I look back at that journal I can see how dominant this 'God' had become in the mind of his self-critical and unworthy servant. However, *and this really blew my mind,* as I looked again at my journal, I saw another voice within my writings... a deeper wiser voice... the voice of the Wizard Within.

I don't want to give the impression that I have a split personality. I am not talking about 'voices' in that sense. I am talking about what I now tend to call the little-me and the Divine-Me, two distinct voices within us all. The little-me corresponds to that *mass of noise* in our heads that often stops us from enjoying any sense of real peace. My 'rituals of repentance' and all the negative stuff I wrote about myself was coming from this little-me, but it's not *just* the negative stuff. I have now begun to realise that the little-me is more than one voice. The little–me is the ego's voice (s) which can be fearful and small, self-punishing and masochistic, angry and defensive, depressive and negative, proud and superior or self-righteous and larger than life. One reason why I prefer to use 'little-me' than ego or (as some say) false self, is that those terms sound rather harsh and negative. They often come from the traditions that say 'fight and kill the ego'. In my experience when you fight something you actually give it more power, and potentially make it bigger, so I would rather take the point of view that says see the ego for what it is... a façade... a mask behind which the real me lives.... By seeing the ego like this, we learn to take its words less seriously and lessen its power. No, the problem is not that we have an ego but that we have allowed it to become so in control and *loud* inside our heads that the deeper wiser voice of the Wizard is hardly detectable. I also call this Wizard the Divine-Me.

I wonder have you ever had this experience? You are trying to work out a particular plan of action and there is a conversation in your head... even an argument perhaps. To put it simply there is one voice telling you to do go one thing, and another voice saying the opposite. Often one is negative and critical and the other more positive and reasonable. Now let's imagine those voices are deep in argument over a public speech you've been asked to give:

> 'Of course you can do it. Stop being such a coward. Grow up and prove you're a man. Come on!'
>> **'No, shut up! What if I make a cock up like last time?'**
> 'Come on. Believe in yourself.'
>> **'No, I can't. They'll laugh at me. They think I'm a jerk...'**

If the *tone* of this mental debate sounds at all familiar then let me ask this, have you ever also had the experience of a *third* voice entering the picture... a voice that, right out of the blue, says:

> *'Shhhh. Peace. Listen to your heart. You <u>can</u> do it... but even if it does go wrong does it really matter? Remember the <u>bigger</u> picture...'*

This is the Wizard's voice. It's deeper than the two arguing voices. It is the inner guide that helps you to KNOW which way to go. Both the first and second voices were little-me voices. The first was like a tough school master; 'Go on boy. You do it. Prove yourself.' The second was whining and pathetic like a spoilt child. I'll admit I can recognise both voices inside my own head at times. The Wizard's voice agreed with the school master *but* was not after an ego trip or a chance to prove anything. It went on to point out that in reality *it really doesn't matter* in the scheme of things. The Wizard can bring a great sense of peace and rest (and I would say magic) if we allow him to have the room to speak.

If this sounds confusing it might help if I use an example from a <u>much</u> cleverer person than me... the great C.S.Lewis. Lewis spoke, in his wonderful book, *Mere Christianity,* about the Moral Law. This is over simplifying considerably but he taught that there are two instincts in every human being, an instinct for right and an instinct for wrong. Some call the former instinct the voice of your conscience. Now Lewis did not see the voice of your conscience as in itself the Moral Law... he saw the Moral Law as something deeper, which lay underneath those two instincts. One example of this, for Lewis, was to imagine a person witnessing someone else drowning in a river. There would probably be two impulses within this person: a stronger impulse of self-protection, and a weaker impulse of risk and rescue. Lewis said that the Moral Law would be *telling the person* to go with the weaker instinct and risk his/her own safety for the sake of another.

It is interesting that, here, C.S.Lewis clearly thought of the Moral Law as in some sense an inner 'voice'.

Now please don't misunderstand me, I'm not saying that Lewis's Moral Law and my Wizard Within are the same thing. I'm simply using the former an example of how a third voice can lie underneath two other influences or voices.

So, if we do all have this inner Wizard how do we access his wisdom and become more aware of his voice? Well the obvious answer to that is meditation and to learn to spend more time in the present moment... *where he lives*, and there are countless excellent books and tapes available on that subject. But on top of that there's one exercise that I have found very helpful. I call it 'Epistles to Ourselves'.

The exercise involves finding a quiet moment and writing a letter to a God (or, if you can't cope with God-language, a letter to the Will of the Universe, the Higher Power etc.) expressing any thoughts, feelings or questions that come to mind. Then, after having had a break, write a reply to yourself *as if from God* (Higher Power etc.).

I must emphasise the words *'as if from'* here. I am **not** claiming that this exercise puts us in touch with God himself. The replies to the letters are *not* modern day Biblical epistles. However, the experience of prayerfully imagining what God might want to say to you can potentially open yourself up to the deeper voice of the Divine-Me / the Wizard Within.

I once set an exercise like this for all the local clergy where I work. I'd been asked to lead a day on 'Priesthood?' I must say, my colleagues were not over eager to carry out my exercise. On the day itself most of us had completed the exercise and the time had come to share the letters. What I observed blew my mind for I began to hear about a completely different God than the one we usually talked about in our clergy Bible studies. It was as if writing these letters had opened us up to another dimension of God.

One priest was visibly surprised by her own words and when she'd finished reading her letter she held it close to her heart and said, 'Oh thank you God'.

Friends the Wizard does exist. Be still, slow down occasionally and listen for him. He is there.

AFTERWORD

This entire story is a work of fiction. No character is based on any real person, neither is the church fellowship to which Sam and his mother belonged. Any correlations are therefore accidental. However the book mentioned in chapter 45 is a real book; one which the author has found to be of extreme value. All other ideas and beliefs are fiction and do not in any way correspond to the beliefs of the author.

Quotations in Chapter 45 – Taken from 'God Calling' Edited by A.J.Russell, Published by O Books, 2006 (first published 1935)

ENDORSEMENTS

Wizards are very much into the proper blending of things, making new creations that lead to old wisdoms, finding new awakening in ancient endeavours. Mark Townsend is such alchemy. Mark is both a Magician and Christian Priest, but don't let that frighten you away. Mark has the unusual drive to find the mysterious in Christianity and to combine both worlds to make a more universal spirituality. His work is unlike the common trend of modern clergy and Christian church. Mark envisions a personal spiritual evolvement with wonder, the miraculous as a natural part of daily life.

Wizards of the modern age still keep many ancient secrets and can hint only at what is within each of us. Wizards provoke students into a journey that leads within. Mark does this beautifully in his novel, and we shall both meet you as you travel there with us.

Kenton Knepper, Wizard and Master of Mysteries

I wish that every person who approaches magic would do it with the same attitude that Mark Townsend's characters show in this engaging book. There is a healthy restlessness, an initial rebellion, in Sam and Jane as they find themselves following their own paths towards magic. This is an uneasiness that is natural. I know because I often feel it myself and I have to assume that Mark, being both a magician and a priest, might feel it too from time to time. Magic, especially in our times, is a foolish thing, as foolish as all fundamental things are because, as André Bretón said, "Only the superfluous is truly indispensable." I think Mark has given us a useful guide for how to feel when we are touched by magic and know we can't keep ignoring it – a guide disguised as a mesmerizing tale that is almost impossible to put down once you start reading it!

Enrique Enriquez, Magician and Metaphorical Mindreader.

Mark book 'The Wizard's Gift' brings wonder back to life, and awakens his readers to the often long forgotten reality of their own inner magic.

Romany - Diva of Magic

BOOKS

O books
O is a symbol of the world, of oneness and unity. In different cultures it also means the "eye", symbolizing knowledge and insight, and in Old English it means "place of love or home". O books explores the many paths of understanding which different traditions have developed down the ages, particularly those today that express respect for the planet and all of life.

For more information on the full list of over 300 titles please visit our website
www.O-books.net

myspiritradio is an exciting web, internet, podcast and mobile phone global broadcast network for all those interested in teaching and learning in the fields of body, mind, spirit and self development. Listeners can hear the show online via computer or mobile phone, and even download their favourite shows to listen to on MP3 players whilst driving, working, or relaxing.

Feed your mind, change your life with O Books, The O Books radio programme carries interviews with most authors, sharing their wisdom on life, the universe and everything...e mail questions and co-create the show with O Books and myspiritradio.

Just visit **www.myspiritradio.com** for more information.